Determinants of Res
– Empirical Analyses of Price Effec

CW00508034

Determinants of Residual Values
– Empirical Analyses of Price Effects in the Used-Car Market

Von der
Carl-Friedrich-Gauß-Fakultät
der Technischen Universität Carolo-Wilhelmina zu Braunschweig

zur Erlangung des Grades eines
Doktors der Wirtschaftswissenschaften (Dr. rer. pol.)

genehmigte Dissertation

von
Sebastian Gutknecht
geboren am 16.04.1986
in Duderstadt

Eingereicht am: 22.08.2019
Disputation am: 12.02.2020
1. Referent: Prof. Dr. Marc Gürtler
2. Referent: Prof. Dr. David M. Woisetschläger

2020

Bibliografische Information der Deutschen Nationalbibliothek
Die Deutsche Nationalbibliothek verzeichnet diese Publikation in der Deutschen
Nationalbibliographie; detaillierte bibliographische Daten sind im Internet über
http://dnb.d-nb.de abrufbar.
1. Aufl. - Göttingen: Cuvillier, 2020
    Zugl.: (TU) Braunschweig, Univ., Diss., 2020

© CUVILLIER VERLAG, Göttingen 2020
    Nonnenstieg 8, 37075 Göttingen
    Telefon: 0551-54724-0
    Telefax: 0551-54724-21
    www.cuvillier.de

    ISBN 978-3-7369-7195-0
    eISBN 978-3-7369-6195-1

Zusammenfassung der Dissertation

Determinants of Residual Values
– Empirical Analyses of Price Effects in the Used-Car Market –

In den vergangenen Jahrzehnten stiegen die Anzahl und die Höhe der Leasinginvestitionen in Deutschland stark an, sodass der Leasingsektor mittlerweile den größten Anteil an den gesamtwirtschaftlichen Investitionen in Deutschland hat. Gerade im Fahrzeugleasing ist diese Entwicklung am ausgeprägtesten zu beobachten. Aus diesem Grund rückt das Restwertrisiko für Fahrzeuge verstärkt in den Fokus vieler Finanzinstitute. Dies beschreibt das Risiko, dass der Wert eines Fahrzeuges am Ende der Leasinglaufzeit unter dem vertraglich vereinbarten Restwert liegt. Ausschlaggebend für die Höhe des Restwertrisikos ist selbstverständlich die Qualität der Restwertprognose. Die Herausforderung bei der Erstellung einer belastbaren Prognose liegt in der Berücksichtigung aller relevanter restwertbeeinflussender Faktoren. Neben gängigen Einflussfaktoren auf den Restwert, wie z. B. Laufleistung, Ausstattung oder Fahrzeugalter, können auch exogene Faktoren einen erheblichen Einfluss haben. Zu diesen zählen z. B. politische Eingriffe wie Subventionen in Form von Abwrackprämien, die zu substanziellen Veränderungen des Angebots und der Nachfrage führen können. Aber auch die Zahlungsbereitschaft zukünftiger potenzieller Käufer der Leasingrückläufer hat einen entscheidenden Einfluss auf den resultierenden Verkaufspreis. Potenzielle Gebrauchtwagenkäufer nutzen i. d. R. keine Modelle um den Verkaufspreis zu bestimmen, sondern orientieren sich an verfügbaren Angeboten im Internet oder anderen Informationsquellen. Aufgrund der Vielzahl an Angeboten kann deren Fahrzeugbewertung durch vereinfachende heuristische Entscheidungsregeln beeinflusst sein und von den rationalen, modellbasierten Prognosen abweichen.

Vor diesem Hintergrund besteht das Ziel der vorliegenden Dissertation darin, restwertbeeinflusse Faktoren zu identifzieren mit dem Schwerpunkt die Auswirkungen limitierter Informationsverarbeitung und exogener Einflussfaktoren auf die Preise von Gebrauchtfahrzeugen zu untersuchen. Dazu wird zunächst ein Literaturüblick über preisdeterminierende Einflussfaktoren von Gebrauchtwagen gegeben. Im weiteren Verlauf dieser Arbeit werden die Auswirkungen von heuristischer Informationsverarbeitung auf die Preise im Sekundärmarkt analysiert. Dabei wird u. a. mit Hilfe eines empirischen Modells untersucht, ob das Ausmaß des Preiseffekts aufgrund heuristischer Informationsverarbeitung von den kognitiven Fähigkeiten und dem Informationsstand der Marktteilnehmer abhängt. Daran anschließend wird untersucht, welchen Einfluss staatliche Interventionen, die zu einem erheblichen Angebots- und Nachfrageschock auf dem Sekundärmarkt führen, auf die Preise von Gebrauchtfahrzeugen haben. Dazu wird in Kapitel 2 zunächst ein Überblick über die Entwicklung und Bedeutung des Automobil- und Leasingmarktes in Deutschland gegeben, da gerade das Fahrzeugleasing aufgrund des hohen und weiter steigenden Marktanteils an den gesamten Leasinginvestitionen in Deutschland von besonderem Interesse ist. Dabei haben Leasingunternehmen, die sich im Besitz von Banken befinden (bankennahe Leasing-Gesellschaften), einen erheblichen Anteil an den gesamten Leasinginvestionen. Zudem liegt das Restwertrisiko im Fahrzeugleasing in der Regel beim Leasinggeber. Von zentraler Bedeutung ist daher die Identifikation relevanter Einflussfaktoren auf die Restwerte der Fahrzeuge. Aus diesem Grund wird in Kapitel 3 ein ausführlicher Literaturüberblick gegeben, der die wesentlichen Preisdeterminanten darstellt. Dabei werden sowohl physische Fahrzeugeigenschaften als auch die Entwicklungen im Automobilmarkt und der Gesamtwirtschaft betrachtet. In Kapitel 4 wird mit Hilfe eines Datensatzes des Online-Gebrauchtwagenportals AutoScout24 nachgewiesen, dass Verkäufer von Gebrauchtwagen bei ihrer Fahrzeugbewertung einer Ankerheuristik unterlegen sind und bei ihrer Fahrzeugbewertung nur das Zulassungsjahr, aber nicht den Zulassungsmonat berücksichtigen. Als Resultat dieser Fehlbewertung kann gezeigt werden, dass Fahrzeuge, die in der ersten Jahreshälfte zugelassen worden sind, im Durchschnitt zu teuer und Fahrzeuge, die in der zweiten Jahreshälfte zugelassen worden sind, im Mittel zu günstig angeboten werden. Somit kann gezeigt werden, dass zwei absolut identische Fahrzeuge, die sich nur in ihrem Zulassungsmonat unterscheiden, einen erheblichen, signifikanten Preisunterschied aufweisen. Zusätzlich kann nachgewiesen werden, dass gewerbliche Händler Kenntnis von dem Vorliegen einer solchen Ankerheuristik haben und das fehlerhafte Preisverhalten von privaten Käufern zu ihrem Vorteil nutzen. Als weiteres Ergebnis kann festgestellt werden, dass der relative Preiseffekt der Ankerheuristik mit steigendem Fahrzeugwert abnimmt. Da Käufer von teuren Fahrzeugen im Mittel einen höheren Bildungsgrad besitzen, impliziert dies, dass der Effekt der heuristischen Informationsverarbeitung mit steigenden kognitiven Fähigkeiten abnimmt. Zusammenfassend kann geschlussfolgert werden, dass der Monat der Erstzulassung einen erheblichen Einfluss auf den Restwert eines Fahrzeuges hat und daher bei den Restwertprognosen Berücksichtigung finden sollte. Im anschließenden Verlauf dieser Dissertation werden exogene Einlussfaktoren auf die Preise von Gebrauchtfahrzeugen bzw. Restwerte empirisch nachgewiesen und detailliert untersucht. Auf Basis zweier Datensätze wird in Kapitel 5 am Beispiel der Abwrackprämie in Deutschland im Jahr 2009 nachgewiesen, dass die Preise von jungen Gebrauchtfahrzeugen aufgrund eines Nachfragerückgangs stark gesunken sind. Die Preise von sehr alten Gebrauchtfahrzeugen hingegen stiegen bedingt durch ein verknapptes Angebot aufgrund der Verschrottung von nahezu zwei Millionen alten Fahrzeugen an. Es kann zudem gezeigt werden, dass der Preiseffekt auch nach dem Ablauf des staatlichen Förderprogramms weiter vorliegt und sich teilweise sogar verstärkt hat. Da Abwrackprämien häufig als politische Maßnahmen zur Stimulierung der wirtschaftlichen Situation eingesetzt werden, sind diese Ergebnisse von hoher Relevanz für Leasingunternehmen, aber auch für Banken, für welche der Wert ihrer Sicherheiten von der Entwicklung am Gebrauchtwagenmarkt abhängt.

Acknowledgement

This dissertation was mainly written during my time as a research associate at the Department of Finance at the Technische Universität Braunschweig and finished after starting my career as a risk manager at Volkswagen AG Group Treasury.

At this point, I would like to thank everyone who contributed to the success of my doctoral thesis. I am grateful to my supervisor, Prof. Dr. Marc Gürtler, for several discussions, critical questions and the freedom to define my scientific research. I also want to thank Prof. Dr. David M. Woisetschläger, who reviewed my thesis.

I spent more than five years at the Department of Finance and would also like to thank the whole team for several discussions and the nice working atmosphere. Especially my officemate Dr. Philipp Neelmeier helped me a lot improving my thesis by numerous critical and helpful discussion. I would also like to thank Dr. Thomas Paulsen and Dr. Piet Usselmann for the good collaboration within the project with Volkswagen FS and lots of discussions related to all kinds of topics.

This thesis would not have been possible without the support of my family. Special thanks go to my parents who support me in all my activities and always believed in me and the success of my work. Thank you very much!

Braunschweig, März 2020

Sebastian Gutknecht

Contents

1 Introduction   **1**

  1.1   Problem Definition and Objective of This Work   1

  1.2   Course of Investigation   3

2 The German Automobile and Leasing Market   **6**

  2.1   Fundamentals of the German Automobile Market   6

  2.2   The German Leasing Market   9

      2.2.1   Definition and Characteristics of the Leasing Business   10

      2.2.2   Forms of Contracts   12

      2.2.3   Structure and Economic Importance of the Leasing Market in Germany   15

3 Determinants of Residual Values: A Literature Review   **20**

  3.1   Fundamentals and Motivation   20

  3.2   Influencing Factors and Characteristics of Residual Values   22

      3.2.1   Determining Vehicles' Depreciation Rate   25

      3.2.2   Car-Specific Depreciation Factors   28

      3.2.3   Time-Dependent Depreciation Factors   38

      3.2.4   Other Residual Value Influencing Factors   50

  3.3   Interim results   53

4 Anchoring and Price Anomalies   **55**

  4.1   Fundamentals and Research Questions   55

  4.2   Literature Review   58

  4.3   Hypotheses   60

  4.4   Description of the Data Set   65

  4.5   Empirical Results   68

      4.5.1   Anchoring in the Used-Car Market   70

      4.5.2   Exploiting Anchoring by Professional Sellers   75

      4.5.3   The Impact of Cognitive Abilities on the Size of the Anchoring Effect   82

4.6 Interim Results 85
4.7 Appendix 87
   4.7.1 Akaike Information Criterion 87
   4.7.2 Price Discontinuities: Robustness Checks 87
   4.7.3 Regression with Discontinuity Design 97

5 The Price Effect of Supply and Demand Shocks on Secondary Markets 98
5.1 Fundamentals and Research Questions 98
5.2 Literature Review 101
5.3 Germany's Scrappage Scheme 104
5.4 Modeling Approach and Hypotheses 108
   5.4.1 Model 108
   5.4.2 Hypotheses 111
      5.4.2.1 Model-based Hypotheses 111
      5.4.2.2 Further Hypotheses 115
5.5 Data and Empirical Strategy 116
   5.5.1 Description of the Data Set 116
   5.5.2 Empirical Strategy 124
5.6 Empirical Results 128
   5.6.1 Price Effect for Small Young Cars 128
   5.6.2 Shortage of Old Clunkers 135
   5.6.3 Price Effects between Dealers' and Private Sales 137
5.7 Robustness Checks 141
   5.7.1 Alternative Reference Group - Price Effects for Small Young Cars 141
   5.7.2 Alternative Reference Group - Shortage of Old Clunkers 144
5.8 Interim Results 145
5.9 Appendix 147
   5.9.1 Difference-in-Differences Estimator 147
   5.9.2 Wald-Test 148

6 Conclusion   **150**

List of Figures

2.1   Developments of the New-Car Registrations and Changes of Ownership in
      Germany (2004-2016)   7
2.2   Sales Volume of the German New-Car Market and Used-Car Market (2004-
      2015)   8
2.3   General Functioning of a Leasing Transaction   10
2.4   Leasing Investments in Billion Euros   16
2.5   Developments of Leasing Quotas   17
2.6   Leasing Objects' Share of the New Business   18
2.7   Costumers' Share of the New Business   18

4.1   Residuals - Registration Year Discontinuities   73
4.2   Price Discrepancy: The Impact of the Month of the Initial Registration .   77
4.3   Robustness Check - Price Discrepancy: The Impact of the Month of the
      Initial Registration   78
4.4   Price Discontinuities at Vintage Thresholds   89

5.1   Monthly New-Car Registrations in Germany (2007-2011)   106
5.2   Monthly New-Car Registrations in Germany for Different Car Classifica-
      tions (2008-2011)   107
5.3   Yearly Sales (Left) and Sales Value (Right) of New Cars and Used Cars in
      Germany   117

List of Tables

2.1 Vehicle Classification by the Commission of the European Communities . 9

3.1 Number of Publications Categorized by Model Types 23
3.2 Number of Publications Categorized by Functional Forms of the Dependent Variable 24
3.3 Number of publications categorized by their modeled depreciation pattern 28
3.4 Number of Publications Categorized by Car-Specific Variables 37
3.5 Number of Publications Categorized by Time-Specific Variables 50
3.6 Number of Publications Categorized by Car Markets 54

4.1 Summary Statistics - Continuous Variables 68
4.2 Summary Statistics - Categorical Variables 69
4.3 Anchoring in the Used-Car Market 74
4.4 Exploiting Anchoring by Professional Sellers 80
4.5 The Influence of Cognitive Ability on Anchoring 83
4.6 The Price Effect of Vintage Discontinuities on Used Cars 91
4.7 Robustness Checks - Vintage Discontinuities: Logarithmized Prices . . . 93
4.8 Robustness Checks - Varying the Order of the Age Polynomial 94
4.9 Robustness Checks - Age Thresholds 96

5.1 Summary Statistics - Continuous Variables 119
5.2 Summary Statistics - Categorical Variables 120
5.3 Average price by vehicle segment 121
5.4 Definition of Clunker 126
5.5 Data Set I: Price Effects for Small Young Cars 129
5.6 Data Set I: Effect of Scrappage for Small Young Cars (DiD) 131
5.7 Data Set II: Effect of Scrappage for Small Young Cars 133
5.8 Data Set II: Effect of Scrappage for Small Young Cars (DiD) 134
5.9 Data Set II: Effect of Scrappage for Clunkers 136

5.10 Data Set II: Effect of Scrappage for Clunkers (DiD) 136

5.11 Data Set II: Effect of Scrappage - Private vs. Dealer 139

5.12 Data Set II: Effect of Scrappage - Private vs. Dealer (DiD) 140

5.13 Robustness Checks: Effect of Scrappage for Small Young Cars 143

5.14 Robustness Checks: Effect of Scrappage for Small Young Cars (DiD) . . . 143

5.15 Robustness Checks: Effect of Scrappage for Clunkers 144

5.16 Robustness Checks: Effect of Scrappage for Clunkers (DiD) 145

5.17 Policy Effect for the Treatment Group and the Control Group 148

Nomenclature

Abbreviations

AIC	Akaike Information Criterion
ARIMA	Autoregressive Integrated Moving Average
BAFA	Federal Office of Economics and Export Control
	(Bundesamt für Wirtschaft und Ausfuhrkontrolle)
BDL	Federation of German Leasing Companies
	(Bundesverband Deutscher Leasing-Unternehmen)
cf.	Confer
DAT	Deutsche Automobil Treuhand
DiD	Difference-in-Differences
EC	European Commission
e.g.	Exempli gratia
et al.	Et alii
etc.	Et cetera
EURIBOR	Euro Interbank Offered Rate
f.	Following page
ff.	Following pages
FIBOR	Frankfurt Interbank Offered Rate
G7	Group of 7
G8	Group of 8
GDP	Gross Domestic Product
HEV	Hybridized Electric Gasoline
IT	Information Technology
KWG	Banking Act
	(Kreditwesengesetz)
LGD	Loss Given Default
Max	Maximum
Min	Minimum

No.	Number
Obs.	Observations
OECD	Organisation for Economic Co-operation and Development
OLS	Ordinary Least Squares
p.	Page
Sd	Standard Deviation
SUV	Sport Utility Vehicle
TDI	Turbocharged Direct Injection
U.S.	United States
Vol.	Volume
vs.	Versus

Mathematical Symbols

$1_{\{\}}$	Indicator variable
a_i	Actual age of car i
C	Control group
c	Constant
D	Indicator variable
$d2$	Indicator variable for the post-policy period
D_i	Indicator variable for explanatory variable i
d_{ij}	Indicator variable for car i and vintage threshold j
dT	Indicator variable for the treatment group
E	Expectation
$f(\cdot)$	Function
	Density
H_0	Null hypothesis
H_1	Alternate hypothesis
h	Number of hypotheses
i	Index
j	Index
k	Clunker
	Number of parameters
$\hat{\mathcal{L}}$	Likelihood function
ln	Natural logarithm
M	Model
$\mathcal{N}(\cdot)$	Standard normal distribution

N_t	Set of all new and used cars at time t
n	Sample size
$n(i)$	Function that indicates the segment of vehicle i
p	Level of significance
$p_{j,t}$	Price of car j at time t
$P(\cdot)$	Probability
p25	0.25-quantile
p50	Median, 0.5-quantile
p75	0.75-quantile
$pgap_i$	Price discrepancy for car i between asking price and adequate car value
$price_i$	Price of car i
$q_{j,t}$	Quality level of car j at time t
R^2	Coefficient of determination
t	Point in time
T	Treatment group
u	Error term
$u_{i,j,t}$	Consumer i's net utility of car j at time t
$\hat{u}(q_j, t)$	Consumer i's utility value of owning car j at time t
Var	Variance
X	Set of covariates
X_i	Covariate i
	Random variable
x_i	Variable
	Realization of the random variable X_i
y	Dependent variable
$\bar{y}_{\cdot,\cdot}$	Average of the dependent variable as a function of the group and time
α	Level of significance
	Constant
α_i	Consumer i's marginal utility from wealth
β	Coefficient vector
β_0	Constant
β_j	Coefficient of independent variable j
$\hat{\beta}$	Estimator of the coefficient vector
$\hat{\beta}_j$	Estimator of the coefficient of independent variable j
γ_i	Vehicle-specific parameter
	Coefficient vector

δ_j	Coefficient of independent variable j
$\hat{\delta}_1$	Difference-in-differences estimator
ϵ_i	Error term of car i
$\epsilon_{i,j,t}$	Error term for consumer i and car j at time t
θ	Parameter
λ_i	Vehicle-specific parameter
μ	Mean value
σ	Standard deviation
τ	Point in time
$\varnothing$	Average

1 Introduction

1.1 Problem Definition and Objective of This Work

In recent decades, the number of leased and financed vehicles steadily increased and the used-car market became more and more important for financial institutions and car manufacturers. In Germany, one third of all newly registered cars were leased in 2015.[1] Due to this development, the residual value risk moved into the focus of financial institutions that are involved in the leasing business. The residual value risk is the risk that at the end of the lease term the value of the leased vehicle differs from the contractual residual value, which was stipulated at the start of the leasing agreement. Beside the residual value risk, the developments of prices in the used-car market can significantly affect the credit risk of banks who participate in vehicle financing. These institutions are interested in the price changes of their underlying vehicles to determine the value of their collaterals and the Loss Given Default (LGD).

To ensure an appropriate residual value risk management, the quality of the residual value forecasts is most important. Hence, an essential challenge for leasing institutes is the identification of all relevant residual-value-influencing factors. Generally, the prediction of residual values focuses on common influencing factors, such as car age, mileage, equipment, etc. However, models' predictions of used cars' future resale values can differ from individuals' willingness to pay because individuals do not necessarily behave rationally or are misguided by simplifying heuristic decision rules during their car's valuation pro-

---

[1]See Federation of German Leasing Companies (2016, p. 26 ff.).

cess. Hence, experienced sellers of used cars may be able to exploit the price discrepancy between their model-based residual value forecasts and individuals' vehicle assessments, whereas less informed sellers and buyers may suffer from their exposedness to heuristic decision rules. For this purpose, it is essential to understand the effect of individuals' limited or heuristic information processing on the prices of used cars.

Furthermore, in recent years, the used-car market is strongly affected by political and corporate intervention such as subsidies or scrappage schemes. Examples for the German car market are the scrappage premium in 2009, a governmental bonus for the purchase of electric vehicles since 2016 and the scrappage premium of automobile manufacturers for diesel cars since 2017. These car purchase programs do not only exist for the German market but are rather a widely used measure in industrial countries.

As a consequence of these common policies or corporate measures, vehicles' residual values will be affected by exogenous shocks of supply or demand. Understanding the impact of such an exogenous effect is of central importance for financial institutions' residual value risk assessment because it can systematically affect a large number of cars in the leasing portfolio at the same time.

Against this background, the most important research questions addressed in this thesis are the following:

- Which factors determine automobiles residual values?
- What is the effect of individuals' heuristic information processing on the prices of used cars?
- How do sellers' levels of experience and cognitive abilities affect the used-car prices?
- What is the price effect of supply and demand shocks by governmental interventions on secondary markets?

The first question is analyzed by a comprehensive literature review. Based on hedonic pricing models, physical characteristics and performance variables that significantly affect automobiles' residual values are presented. Subsequently, other relevant price determinants are introduced such as macro-economic factors and characteristics of the automobile market. The other three research questions are studied by empirical analyses. The second and the third research questions are analyzed in an empirical project, which considers that sellers' vehicle valuation is subjected to a heuristic called anchoring and identifies the discrepancy between individuals' price assessments and rational market prices. The fourth research question is investigated by analyzing the effect of the German scrappage scheme, which was introduced in 2009, on the prices of used cars. Both empirical projects further examine the price reaction of the studied effects for heterogeneous seller types regarding their levels of information and knowledge.

The results are beneficial for various market participants. Among others, financial institutions have to implement an adequate forecast model for the residual values of their leased vehicles. Taking into account all relevant price-influencing determinants is therefore an important key factor. Thereby, the price effects of a scrappage scheme and individuals' limited information processing are of particular interest to ensure a proper valuation of their risk capital and a quick reaction to market changes. Governments are also interested in the evaluation of their policy measures' price effects because this analysis enables them to understand the corresponding welfare effects. Finally, the results provide simple guidelines for buyers and sellers of both new and used cars and help to reduce the bias caused by heuristic information processing.

1.2 Course of Investigation

To analyze the research questions stated above, this thesis is structured as follows: In Chapter 2, fundamentals of the German automobile market are discussed. First, the German new-car market and used-car market are presented in Section 2.1 to illustrate the importance of the automobile market. In the following Section, an overview about the German leasing market is given. Besides the definition and characteristics of leasing, different contract types are introduced. The last part of this chapter deals with the structure and economic importance of the leasing market in Germany.

In Chapter 3, a detailed analysis of determinants that significantly affect vehicles' residual values is given, which have to be implemented in residual value forecast models to ensure an appropriate prediction of automobiles' resale values. First, the fundamentals and a motivation are given in Section 3.1. Next, a literature review is presented in Section 3.2. In Section 3.2.1, it begins with various studies that investigate the depreciation rate and devaluation pattern of automobiles over the lifetime more generally. Subsequently, in Section 3.2.2, car-specific influencing factors are presented that are analyzed by hedonic pricing models. Besides the impact of physical variables, the effect of performance indicators and the car brand on secondary-market prices are investigated. Section 3.2.3 presents the effects of time-dependent price determinant, which are characterized by the developments in the automobile and the overall market. In Section 3.2.4, other influencing factors are introduced. In the focus of this section are demographic factors and consumer-specific characteristics such as the level of information and their effects on the prices of used vehicles. The main results of this chapter are subsumed in Section 3.3.

The empirical setting of Chapter 4 investigates anchoring and price anomalies in the used-car market. The main focus of this chapter is to examine the price effects of individuals' heuristic information processing. Due to the great required effort to evaluate all relevant car information, individuals often base their pricing on simplifying decision rules, which cause price discrepancies between individuals' car valuation and adequate market values. Again, at first, the fundamentals and research questions of this chapter are presented (cf. Section 4.1). Afterwards, a literature review about price effects of heuristic information processing is given in Section 4.2. In Section 4.3, the hypotheses of this empirical study are derived. An overview about the data set is provided in Section 4.4. The empirical study itself is in the focus of Section 4.5. First, price discontinuities, which are the result of individuals' exposedness to anchoring on the average car value of similar cars from the same vintage, are identified in the used-car market. Then, the size of the anchoring effect with respect to sellers' levels of experience and cognitive abilities are investigated. The main results of this chapter are summarized in Section 4.6.

The empirical analyses in Chapter 5 determines the price effects of supply and demand shocks on secondary markets. These shocks can be a result from governmental interventions such as the scrappage scheme in Germany in 2009, which is the analyzed event in this chapter. The fundamentals and research questions are presented in Section 5.1. A literature review about the effect of governmental intervention on the automobile market with a focus on new-car sales, manufacturer benefits and the competitiveness and welfare effects of secondary markets is given in Section 5.2. Section 5.3 gives a detailed overview about the scrappage program in Germany in 2009 and its progress. In Section 5.4, a theoretical model is implemented, which is used to derive the hypotheses of this empirical study. An overview about the data sets and the empirical strategy is given in Section 5.5. First, two different data sets used in the upcoming analyses are presented. Second, a description of the empirical strategy is provided. The empirical results regarding the price effects of a demand shock of young and small used cars and of a supply shock of old clunkers are established in Section 5.6. In addition, price effects between dealers' and private sales are analyzed in detail. Section 5.7 provides robustness checks. The key findings of this chapter are summarized in Section 5.8.

Finally, Chapter 6 summarizes the results of the preceding chapters and addresses the importance of their consideration for an appropriate residual value risk management.

2 The German Automobile and Leasing Market

2.1 Fundamentals of the German Automobile Market

In this section, an overview about the German automobile market is provided. The stock of passenger cars has constantly increased in recent years and reached 45.1 millions cars in 2016 (41.1 million cars in 2008).[2] In Germany, on average, each household has more than one car. This shows the high relevance of the automobile market in Germany and emphasize the importance of an understanding of the developments and the current situation in this market for the German population and the German economy.[3] The automobile market can be divided into the new-car market and the used-car market. The importance of both markets can be illustrated by the developments of the yearly new-car registrations and changes of ownership, which are presented in Figure 2.1.

The numbers of new-car registrations were relatively constant over the years 2004 to 2016 and reached approximately 3.2 million cars on average. Noticeably, the numbers of new-car registrations increased to 3.8 million cars in 2009 as a result of the introduction of the German scrappage scheme in the same year. This policy measure was implemented because of decreasing new-car sales as a consequence of the financial crisis

---

[2] According to Federal Motor Transport Authority (2016).
[3] This is not only a typical characteristic of the German automobile market but rather a general fact for all developed countries. See Lock (2003), White (2016) and International Organization of Motor Vehicle Manufacturers (2017).

Figure 2.1: **Developments of the New-Car Registrations and Changes of Ownership in Germany (2004-2016)**
Source: Federal Motor Transport Authority (2017a) and Federal Motor Transport Authority (2017b).

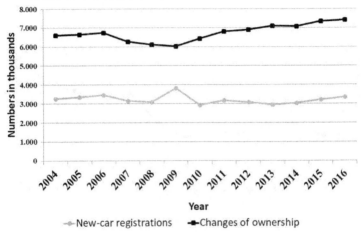

of 2007-2008 and is analyzed in detail in Chapter 5. During the years 2014 to 2016 the new-car registrations slightly increased.

Since 2009, the numbers of changes of ownership increased from 6 million to 7.4 million. Again, the low numbers in 2009 can be explained by the introduction of the scrappage scheme but also by the impacts of the great depression, which began in 2007. As a result, the numbers of changes of ownership decreased during the years 2007 to 2009. However, the strong growth of the numbers of changes of ownerships in recent years emphasize the increasing importance of the used-car market. Hence, a detailed analysis of the functioning and price formation process in the used-car market is necessary to be able to react to changes in supply and demand.

The growing importance of the used-car market is also underlined by the developments of the used cars' sales volume. In Figure 2.2 the sales volume of new and used cars in the years 2004 to 2015 are presented.

Figure 2.2: **Sales Volume of the German New-Car Market and Used-Car Market (2004-2015)**
Source: Deutsche Automobil Treuhand (2016, p. 79).

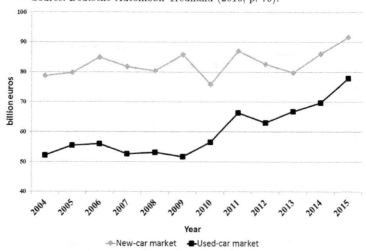

Whereas the new-car sales volume was relatively constant over the last years, the used-car sales volume strongly increased since 2010. The volume of used-car sales was approximately 51.7 billion euros in 2009 and increased to 77.9 billion euros in 2015. Hence, the used-car sales volume came closer to the sales volume level of new cars, which is the result of the increasing numbers of changes of ownership as shown in Figure 2.1.

The new-car registrations are dominated by commercial buyers, which have a market share of more than 66% in 2016. Most new cars were produced by German car manufacturers, which have a share of approximately 64.9% of the total vehicle stock in Germany. Using the car classifications of the European Commission to categorize the car models into the corresponding market segments,[4] the largest-volume car segments are medium cars, small cars and large cars, which make up 26.4%, 19.7% and 15.7% of the existing vehicles in Germany, respectively. Despite the increasing numbers of new registrations of

---

[4]Refer to European Commission (2002).

Sport Utility Vehicles (SUVs), their share of the German vehicle stock is only 8%.[5] Table
2.1 lists the car classifications of the European Commission:

Table 2.1: **Vehicle Classification by the Commission of the European Communities**
The right column lists the three car models for each car classification which had the highest new-registration numbers in 2014 according to the Federal Motor Transport Authority.

Vehicle Classification	Models with highest new-registration numbers
A: mini cars	VW up!, Fiat 500, Opel Adam
B: small cars	VW Polo, Opel Corsa, Ford Fiesta
C: medium cars	VW Golf, Audi A3, Skoda Octavia
D: large cars	VW Passat, Mercedes C-Class, BMW 3 Series
E: executive cars	Audi A6, BMW 5 Series, Mercedes E-Class
F: luxury cars	Mercedes S-Class, Mercedes CLS, Audi A8
J: sport utility cars	VW Tiguan, Opel Mokka, Ford Kuga
S: sport coupes	Mercedes E-Class Coupe, Porsche 911, Mercedes SLK
M: multi-purpose cars	VW Touran, VW Transporter, VW Caddy

The right column of Table 2.1 presents the three car models that yielded the largest numbers of new registrations in 2014 for each car classification.

2.2 The German Leasing Market

This section provides insights into the leasing business and gives an overview about the German leasing market. The leasing industry is particularly affected by the developments in the secondary markets because leasing companies usually have to resale their leased goods at the end of the leasing contract. Hence, leasing companies are challenged to correctly assess the market value of their leased good at the end of the lease term. Only a correct valuation of the leased assets at the end of the contract period ensures the leasing institute's competitiveness and the prevention of future losses. In the remainder of this chapter, a short introduction into the leasing business is given and a typical leasing

---

[5]See Federal Motor Transport Authority (2017c).

transaction is presented. Subsequently, different contract forms and their characteristics
are explained. Finally, the structure and the economic importance of the German leasing
market is demonstrated.

2.2.1 Definition and Characteristics of the Leasing Business

Generally, leasing can be defined as an object's transfer of use in return for a regular payment for a limited period of time. Typically, leasing objects are capital goods or durable
consumer goods, which have economic value and can be used separately.[6] However, a
uniform definition does not exist in the literature. Many characteristics of the leasing
business are similar to the rental business but there are also some properties which are
more related to credit financing. To illustrate the fundamental functionality of the leasing
business, Figure 2.3 presents the involved parties of a typical leasing transaction including
the dependencies between each other.

Figure 2.3: **General Functioning of a Leasing Transaction**[7]

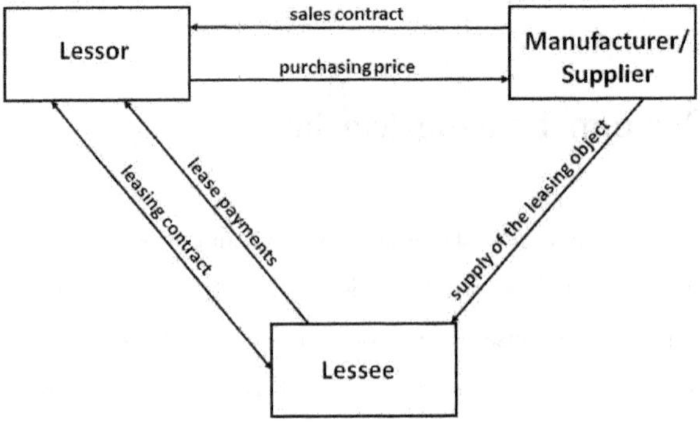

Before the conclusion of the leasing contract, the lessee specifies the desired configuration of the required leasing object. For example, in the case of vehicle leasing, this

---

[6]See Das (2009, p. 125 ff.).
[7]According to Kratzer and Kreuzmair (2002, p. 82).

can be the yearly mileage, the color of the car or the engine power. The price of the leased object is therefore not explicitly given by the lessor, but depends on the lessee's individual equipment features and personal configurations. If the lessee decides to lease the required object, a leasing contract between the lessee and the lessor will be made, where the monthly leasing payments and the contract term will be specified. In the next step, the lessor concludes a sales contract with the manufacturer of the leasing object and pays the agreed purchase price upon delivery. Finally, the leasing object is provided for its use to the lessee, who has to pay the contractual monthly leasing rates to the lessor. The leasing rates ensure the amortization of the lessor's incurred cost, cover the value loss of the leased good over the contract term and include an additional profit margin. During the complete leasing period, the lessor always remains the owner of the leased object.[8]

As already mentioned, leasing transactions show similarities to the rental business and have also some characteristics that are more in line with credit financing. The main differences between the leasing and the rental business is that the lessor is not in possession of the leasing object before the contract conclusion. Moreover, the lessee can determine the specific form of the leasing agreement and the configuration of the leased object. This is similar to credit financing because the borrower can individually chose the investment object and the purchase of this object does not affect the borrower's liquidity position. However, the main difference between leasing and financing is that the lessee does not become the owner of the leased object, whereas the borrower is the legal owner of the purchased good. Moreover, there does not exist an economic relationship between the lender and the manufacturer of the good.[9]

After a short presentation of the general functioning of a leasing transaction, the following section gives an overview about various forms of contracts used in the leasing sector. A basic understanding of the different contract forms is important to be able to distinguish leasing transactions that contain a residual value risk for the leasing company from those that do not.

---

[8]See Kratzer and Kreuzmair (2002, p. 41 ff., p. 82) and Das (2009, p. 129 f.).
[9]See Kratzer and Kreuzmair (2002, p. 16) and Das (2009, p. 128 f.).

2.2.2 Forms of Contracts

Basically, leasing contracts can be classified into two major categories regarding the assignment of the investment risk: finance leasing and operate leasing contracts.[10] Operate leasing contracts are short to medium-term agreements. The lessee has the right of a possible termination of the leasing contract at any time and the leasing company takes the investment risk. For these reasons, the leasing object has to be a durable good that shows relatively high value retention because the lessor's investment costs can only be amortized after multiple leasing arrangements.[11] Typical examples are office buildings, containers or motor vehicles.

In contrast, finance leasing contracts are usually medium to long-term in nature and transfer the investment risk on the lessee's side. Financial leasing contracts are not terminable and can be divided into full amortization contracts and partial amortization agreements.[12] The lessee's leasing payments cover the lessor's costs and risks and additionally contain a profit margin. However, for partial amortization agreements the leasing payments during the lease term only represent a part of the lessor's investment costs. The outstanding amount is determined by the liquidation of the leasing object at the end of the contract term. Depending on the form of the contract, the lessee or the lessor has to bear the risk that the liquidation value of the leasing object is below the contractual residual value.[13]

Financial leasing contracts have a share of approximately 55% of all movable assets' leasing transaction.[14] Car leasing is dominated by finance leasing contracts in the form of partial amortization agreements. Hence, because of the thematic focus of this thesis, in the following, only these contracts are explained in more detail. From the lessee's

---

[10]See Das (2009, p. 130 ff.).
[11]See Kratzer and Kreuzmair (2002, p. 54 ff.).
[12]See Heyd (2008, p. 5 f.).
[13]See Tacke (1999, p. 14 ff.) and Das (2009, p. 135 f.).
[14]See Federation of German Leasing Companies (2016, p. 31).

point of view, financial leasing is primarily used as an financing alternative.[15] For leasing companies that are closer to manufacturers it is an effective sales promotion instrument.[16]

For tax reasons, leasing contracts have to be differentiated regarding their consistence with the leasing decrees in Germany.[17] These decrees regulate under which conditions the leasing object is fiscally attributable to the lessor. According to the partial amortization decree for leasing of moveable goods, which was enacted on December 22, 1975, the minimum lease term for a lease contract must be between 40% and 90% of the usual operating life expectancy. The economic ownership of the leased objects is attributed to the lessor and the leasing contract is not terminable. This decree concerns the regulation of leasing contracts that contain the right for the lessor to sell the leased object to the lessee at the expiration of the contract term, terminable leasing contracts with a final payment and contracts that contain a guaranteed residual value by the lessee and a sharing of excess proceeds.[18] The last mentioned contract type and kilometers-based leasing agreements are established contract types in the market for vehicle leasing.[19]

For lease contracts that contain a put option for the lessor, the leasing company has the right to sell the leasing object to the lessee at the end of the contract term. When the option is exercised, the lessee is obliged to pay the contractual agreed residual value to the lessor. Hence, the lessee bears the residual value risk. In the case of a contract extension, this is not applicable. The lessee has not the right to purchase the leasing object at the contract's expiration date.

Subject to the applicable notice period, for terminable contracts with final payment, the lessee has the option to cancel the agreement upon expiry of the basic rental period. The final payment, which becomes due at the date of termination, ensures the full amortization of the lessor's investments. Up to 90% of the realized proceeds can be taken into account for this payment. If the chargeable amount of the sales proceeds plus the paid leasing rates are below the total costs of the lessor, the lessee has to pay the deficit. In the case

---

[15]See Kraemer-Eis and Lang (2012, p. 11 ff.).
[16]See Tacke (1999, p. 35).
[17]See Reinking (2012, p. 14).
[18]See Reinking and Eggert (2014, p. 1157).
[19]See Santelmann and Mehrgott (2012, p. 61 f.).

that the sales proceeds are greater than the difference of the total costs and the obtained lease payments, the lessor retains the full extent of the sales proceeds.

For contracts that contain a guaranteed residual value by the lessee and a sharing of excess proceeds, the lessee has to return the leasing object to the lessor at the end of the contract term. The lessor has to liquidate the lease return. In the case that the realized proceeds are lower than the calculated residual value, the lessee has to compensate the lessor. If the lessor's proceeds are greater than the residual value, the lessee will obtain a proportion of 25% of the difference between the realized proceeds and the contractual residual value.[20]

For vehicle leasing, the dominating contract form is based on the mileage during the contract period. This contract form is a variation of partial amortization agreements with participation at the excess proceeds, where the leasing company has to bear the risk of the leased object's realized proceeds at the end of the contract term. The basis of these kilometer-based contracts is the contractual agreed mileage of the car during the leasing period. The leasing payments amortize the expected car's loss in value and contain profit margins and risk premiums for the lessor because of the uncertainty of the predicted residual value at the end of the lease term. Upon expiration of the leasing period, the concerned party will be compensated for excess or unused kilometers resulting from the difference between contractual and actual kilometers.[21]

Kilometers-based leasing agreements transfer the residual value risk on the side of the leasing company and are gaining more and more popularity. The lessor is only compensated for the driven kilometers that exceed the contractual agreed mileage. Hence, it is essential for the leasing company to provide accurate residual value forecasts because they will not be compensated for the difference between the expected market value at the conclusion of the contract and the actual market value at the end of the lease term. The contractual residual value determines the amount of the leasing rate. Contractual residual values that are too low, result in high leasing payments for the lessee and a small

---

[20]See Reinking and Eggert (2014, p. 1157 f.).
[21]See Reinking and Eggert (2014, p. 1159).

residual value risk of the lessor, but reduce the lessor's competitiveness in the leasing market.

The market situation at the end of the lease term and the development of the economic environment are uncertain from the perspective of the beginning of the lease term. For this reason and because of the high and growing market share of independent and bank-related leasing companies, an adequate risk management becomes more and more important for leasing companies to safeguard against losses, which may result from a potential deterioration of the prices in the used-car market.[22] In Chapter 3 several influencing factors of used-cars' residual values are presented to ensure an appropriate residual value risk assessment.

2.2.3 Structure and Economic Importance of the Leasing Market in Germany

Since the foundation of the 'Deutsche Leasing GmbH', the first leasing company in Germany in the year 1962, the leasing market shows an increasing development over the last decades and became a more and more important financing alternative.[23] Generally, the leasing objects can be categorized into moveables and real estate. After the UK, Germany is the second largest leasing market in the world.[24] Figure 2.4 presents the development of the leasing investments in Germany during the years 1991 to 2016.

The total leasing investments increased from 26.65 billion euros in 1991 to 58.50 billion euros in 2016. Noticeably, this increasing amount of the leasing investments is the result of movable asset leasing. Except of the break in the years 2009, the investment amount in movables follows a positive trend. The small amount in 2009 may be a result of the economic crisis and the introduction of the scrappage premium, which will be analyzed in Chapter 5. In contrast to the investments of movable assets, the leasing investments

---

[22]See Federation of German Leasing Companies (2016, p. 28).
[23]See Martinek et al. (2008, p. 10) and Städtler (2014, p. 2 ff.).
[24]See Leaseeurope (2015).

Figure 2.4: **Leasing Investments in Billion Euros**
Source: Federation of German Leasing Companies (2017).

in real estate are only of a small amount (1.7 billion euros in 2016) and decreasing in the
last years.

The leasing industry is Germany's largest investor and generates a leasing quota of
16.2% of the total investments in Germany in 2016. For movable assets, the leasing quota
is even significantly higher and corresponds to 24%. In the same year, approximately 1.8
million leasing contracts were concluded. Figure 2.5 illustrates the developments of the
leasing quotas during the years 1991 to 2016.

All in all, the leasing quotas increased during the observed time period. Whereas the
leasing quota of total investments is relatively constant in recent years, the leasing quota
of movable assets still increased in the period between 2010 and 2016. Hence, the developments of both the leasing investments and the leasing quotas highlight the importance
of the leasing market of movable assets.

As presented in Figure 2.6, in Germany, 97% of all leased objects were movables in
2016. The share of real estate leasing was only 3%. With approximately 75%, road vehicles

Figure 2.5: **Developments of Leasing Quotas**
Source: Federation of German Leasing Companies (2017).

had the largest share followed by production machines (10%) and office machines and computer systems (6%). Other movables had only a share of 8%.

The demand side for the leasing objects can be roughly divided into three different types: Commercial customers, private customers and the government. As illustrated by Figure 2.7, their share of the movables' new business was 86%, 12% and 2% in the year 2016, respectively.

The supply side can be characterized by independent, bank-related and manufacturer-related leasing companies. According to the members of the federation of German leasing companies (Bund Deutscher Leasing-Unternehmen, BDL), most leasing companies are independent (54%). Only 26% of all leasing companies are bank-related and 20% are manufacturer-related. However, their share of the movables' new business is much different. Manufacturer-related leasing companies accounted for the largest share (58%), followed by bank-related (32%) and independent leasing companies (10%).[25]

---

[25]See Federation of German Leasing Companies (2016, p. 49).

Figure 2.6: **Leasing Objects' Share of the New Business**
Source: Federation of German Leasing Companies (2016, p. 29).

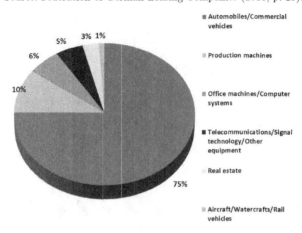

Figure 2.7: **Costumers' Share of the New Business**
Source: Federation of German Leasing Companies (2016, p. 30).

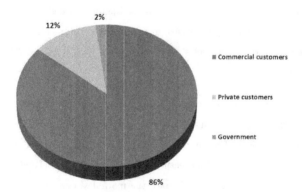

In summary, it can be stated that the German automobile market and leasing market have a significant contribution to the overall German economy, which is still increasing. The importance of the leasing sector is a result of vehicle leasing, which has the largest share of all leasing investments. Approximately one third of all new registrations are leased vehicles.[26] Typically for vehicle leasing contracts, the residual value risk, which arise at the end of the contract term, is transferred to the lessor. Bank-related leasing companies have a considerable part at the leasing business and are subjected to the requirements of the Banking Act (Kreditwesengesetz, KWG) and Basel III. Hence, these leasing companies are obliged to implement an appropriate risk management to cover the residual value risks of their leasing portfolios. For this purpose, it is essential to identify all relevant determinants that affect the prices in the used-car market. Against this background, in the next chapter, an overview about the current literature regarding influencing factors of vehicles' residual values is given.

---

[26]See Federation of German Leasing Companies (2016, p. 28).

3 Determinants of Residual Values: A Literature Review

3.1 Fundamentals and Motivation

Automobiles are durable goods that have economic useful lives of several years. For instance, in Germany, according to the German Federal Motor Transport Authority, approximately 30 percent of all vehicles that were deregistered from public roads in 2017 were older than 15 years.[27] During their utilization period due to normal aging and usual wear and tear vehicles loose in value until they will be scrapped and leave the used-car market.

As seen in Section 2, the second-hand car market has a large volume and the number of used-car transactions significantly exceeds the number of transactions of new vehicles. The importance of the automobile market is determined by people's need for mobility and flexibility. For instance, in Germany, each household has on average more than one car.[28] Similar demand for used vehicles is observable for all industrialized countries. In the United States, China and Japan, the vehicle stock is even larger than in Germany.

---

[27]Statistics about the deregistration number of vehicles can be found on the website of the German Federal Motor Transport Authority: https://www.kba.de/DE/Statistik/Fahrzeuge/Ausserbetriebsetzungen/ausserbetriebsetzungen_node.html#rechts; last accessed: December 31, 2018.

[28]Detailed information about the distribution of automobiles in Germany can be found on the website of the German Federal Statistical Office: https://www.destatis.de/DE/ZahlenFakten/GesellschaftStaat/EinkommenKonsumLebensbedingungen/AusstattungGebrauchsguetern/Tabellen/Fahrzeuge_D.html; last accessed: December 31, 2018.

For instance, the used-vehicle sales in the U.S. reached an all-time high of 39.2 million vehicles in 2017.[29] Hence, the question of how to correctly valuate used automobiles is attracting great interest for both the buyer side as well as the seller side. Especially for leasing companies and automobile banks, there exists a high risk potential due to large concentrations of their portfolio to value developments of used cars. This risk is known as residual value risk.[30]

More specifically, the residual value risk is defined as the risk that the value of the leased asset at the end of the lease term is less than the contractual residual value, which was estimated at the beginning of the contract. Because of unexpected price developments in the secondary market or the sales policy of the leasing institute, the contractual residual value can differ from the leasing object's market value at the end of the leasing term. According to the contractual form, the lessee, the lessor or a third party (e.g. a car manufacturer or car dealer) are exposed to the residual value risk. Some contract forms include a put option for the lessor or a call option for the lessee at the end of the contract period, which contains the right to sell the car to the lessee or to buy the car from the lessor at a contractual agreed price, respectively.

As a consequence of the resulting concentration of residual value risk, an adequate forecast of the value of their leased vehicles is of major importance for leasing companies and banks that are exposed to the value development of used automobiles.[31] However, in a first step, the identification of factors that influence the value of used vehicles is a major challenge. Many studies focus on the question which factors affect automobiles' residual values and investigate vehicles' depreciation pattern. Using multi-factor models, physical characteristics, macro-economic developments and demographic factors are taken into account to explain the second-hand car prices.

---

[29]Statistics can be found on the website of Edmunds, a leading car information and shopping platform: `https://www.edmunds.com/about/press/used-vehicle-sales-hit-record-high-in-2017-according-to-latest-edmunds-used-car-report.html`; last accessed: December 31, 2018.
[30]See Section 2.2.2.
[31]For an overview about forecast models see Rode et al. (2002), Cheng and Wu (2006), Smith and Jin (2007) and Wu et al. (2009).

This chapter is structured as follows: Subsequently to the motivation of the identification of relevant factors that influence residual values of cars, a literature review about the current state of research is given.[32] The literature review is divided into four main parts. In the first part, the literature about the nature and pattern of the depreciation of cars is presented (cf. Section 3.2.1). Studies covering this research topic focus on the analysis of depreciation rates. Another research stream in the literature analyzes car-specific and manufacturer-specific influencing factors of residual values (cf. Section 3.2.2). Generally, these studies consider hedonic pricing approaches to explain the price effect of, for example, car equipment, engine power, color, etc. In most studies, this is done by multiple linear regression models. The third part of the literature analyzing determinants of vehicles' residual values focuses on external market factors and macro-economic factors that are used as an approximation of demand and supply in the used-car market (cf. Section 3.2.3). In Section 3.2.4, other determinants that influence the prices in the second-hand automobile market are considered. Section 3.3 concludes.

3.2 Influencing Factors and Characteristics of Residual Values

This section provides a literature review about influencing factors and characteristics of residual values. In the literature, different approaches for the identification of used-car prices' influencing factors are proposed. Table 3.1 lists the common model types used in research papers and summarizes their number of applications. For this purpose, 33 research papers of the following literature review, which are used as a theoretical foundation of this work, are categorized into their applied models. Obviously, almost all modeling approaches are based on linear regression models. The basic principle of this approach is to explain the used-car price by breaking down the vehicle into its constituent characteristics and obtain estimates of the contributory value of each characteristic. Further specifications consider the market developments and demographic effects. This is done

---
[32]See also Nau (2012).

by regression with ARIMA expectation, difference-in-differences regression and an AR-MAX time series regression model, which are specifications of the linear regression model. Only three studies do not apply the linear regression approach, but use parametric and non-parametric tests to identify vehicles' depreciation pattern.

Table 3.1: **Number of Publications Categorized by Model Types**

Model approach	#
OLS regression	30
Specifications:	
Regression with ARIMA expectation	1
Difference-in-differences regression	1
ARMAX time series regression model	1
(Non-)Parametric tests	3

The first approaches in the literature concentrate on the nature and pattern of the depreciation of vehicles to estimate cars' depreciation rates. Previous research focuses on simple models that explain the price of a car i as a function of car age:

$$log(price_i) = f(a_i) + \epsilon_i, \tag{3.1}$$

where $price_i$ corresponds to the price of car i and $f(a_i)$ stands for a function of the car age a_i. The variable ϵ_i is an error term. Using observable market data of the car prices and car age, the challenge is to estimate an adequate function $f(a_i)$ that explains the depreciation pattern of used cars in a appropriate way. A semi-logarithmic regression approach (log-level model) is applied that uses the logarithmic car price as the response variable. The application of functional forms involving the logarithm of the dependent variable results from the findings of the literature review. Table 3.2 shows that in most research papers the logarithmic used-car price is chosen as the dependent variable. Other studies consider the used-car price directly or focus on relative prices (proportion of the actual price at the original price) and price changes resulting from the vehicle price of the previous year.

Table 3.2: **Number of Publications Categorized by Functional Forms of the Dependent Variable**

Dependent variable	#
Price	10
Log Price	15
Relative Price	5
Log Relative Price	2
Price depreciation (previous year)	1

Section 3.2.1 introduces the existing literature that strives to estimate vehicles' depreciation pattern.

On this basis, Section 3.2.2 presents the literature that extends the simple depreciation model (Equation 3.1). There, several studies analyze the effect of car-specific characteristics on the value of used cars. In most cases, this is done by a multiple regression model of the following form:

$$log(price_i) = \alpha + f(a_i) + \beta'X_i + \epsilon_i, \tag{3.2}$$

where X_i contains the relevant characteristics of car i. For instance, this vector can consist of the car's engine power, the driven kilometers, a dummy variable of the color, etc. Again, based on the findings of Table 3.2, the logarithmic used-car price is applied as the dependent variable. The car characteristics X_i of car i are used as the independent variables of the regression approach. The regression coefficients describe the effect of the respective independent variables and the error term ϵ_i contains all price discrepancies of car i that are not covered by the vector X_i and the other components of the regression equation.

Further model specifications in the literature also consider macro-economic effects on the prices of used cars by extending the model determined by Equation 3.2 to

$$log(price_{i,t}) = \alpha + f(a_i) + \beta'X_i + \gamma'Y_t + \epsilon_{i,t}. \tag{3.3}$$

The vector Y_t contains time-specific variables such as macro-economic factors, which describe the country's economic situation at the time of sale or the car's life cycle. The coefficients α, β and γ can be estimated from observed used-car sales. Section 3.2.3 presents the studies that incorporate time-depending effects on the prices of used cars.

3.2.1 Determining Vehicles' Depreciation Rate

In the focus of the residual value analysis is the mathematical form of the vehicles' depreciation over the life cycle, which can be used as an essential basis for a realistic residual value risk forecast. In this section, different studies that analyze the depreciation pattern of cars are presented. The results can be used as a starting point to determine cars' residual values. In subsequent analyses of residual values' influencing factors these depreciation patterns can be further specified, which may lead to changes and shifts of the basic depreciation curve.

A foundation for the evaluation of vehicles' depreciation rates can be found in Wykoff (1970). In this study, based on a data set of ten different car models of the U.S. automobile market from 1950 to 1969 and nine other car models which have been introduced in the United States in that period, Wykoff (1970) tests three different hypotheses regarding the depreciation pattern of cars. In a first step, the hypothesis that cars depreciation rates are fixed over time is tested. This would indicate that the car value decreases independently over time and the depreciation is not affected by technical progress and other exogenous factors.[33] On the basis of the employed data set, the first hypothesis cannot be rejected although the statistical evidence is rather weak. This result implies that there is no evidence of a changing depreciation pattern over time. In a second step, Wykoff (1970) analyzes whether the depreciation pattern is exponential. The hypothesis that depreciation rates are exponential is rejected. The depreciation in the first year is much higher than an exponential pattern would suggest. However, for cars older than one year an exponential depreciation pattern cannot be rejected. In the last step, Wykoff (1970) analyzes whether the depreciation rates differ between different makes, models

---

[33]See Wykoff (1970, p. 170 f.).

and bodyworks. He finds that the depreciation rates do not show a homogenous pattern
and vary between makes and models. It is noteworthy that in comparison to the other
car models the values of station wagons and imported cars of the small car segment are
relatively stable in their values.

The findings of exponential depreciation rates are confirmed by Bennett (1967) and
Ackerman (1973). Bennett (1967) analyzes the consumption of automobiles in the United
States in the years 1955-1957. By least square estimation techniques he finds that the
automobiles' depreciation pattern fits an exponential form.[34] Using a data set of six
different makes of the U.S. automobile market from 1954 to 1963, Ackerman (1973)
shows that prices of used cars decline with age at a constant exponential depreciation
rate.

In their analysis of the U.S. car market, Ohta and Griliches (1976) contribute to the
results of Wykoff (1970). They analyze the prices of new and used cars of thirteen makes
from the model years 1955 through 1971.[35] Using regression analyses, Ohta and Griliches
(1976) find that the depreciation pattern of used cars differs across different makes and
is not stable over time.[36] As a result, it can be stated that cars' depreciation rates are
time dependent, which differs from the findings regarding the first hypothesis of Wykoff
(1970). However, the observation of make-specific depreciation pattern is in line with the
findings of Wykoff (1970). Additionally, Ohta and Griliches (1976) find evidence for an
exponential depreciation pattern on a five percent significance level for the year 1971,
which confirms the results of Wykoff (1970) and Ackerman (1973). However, Ohta and
Griliches (1976) reveal systematic deviations of the exponential depreciation path as well.
Statistical significant deviations are detectable for six year old cars of the year 1967. They
conclude that actual depreciation occurs at a higher rate with age. Moreover, because of
the great value loss in the first year, the depreciation rate has to be modeled separately
for this time period. Hence, Ohta and Griliches (1976) suggest to handle their empirical

---

[34]See Bennett (1967, p. 842).
[35]See Ohta and Griliches (1976, p. 340 f.).
[36]See Ohta and Griliches (1976, p. 353 ff.).

results with caution: on average, the exponential depreciation pattern can be used as an approximation although this may be rejected for large samples.[37]

Focusing on the depreciation pattern of used cars, Peles (1988) uses a data set of average used-car prices of 34 different models of the U.S. market during the years 1975 to 1985. New cars were excluded as well as cars older than ten years. Peles (1988) tests the best fit of the depreciation pattern of three different approaches steaming from the economic and accounting literature. In the so called one-hoss shay approach, an increasing depreciation rate over time is assumed, whereas the other two accounting-based approaches apply constant or decreasing depreciation rates over time. According to the used sample data, the first approach that applies increasing depreciation rates cannot be confirmed. Instead, both the straight line and declining depreciation rate approach obtain good results. In the last step, Peles (1988) implements a regression model that includes both a linear and an exponential term to model the depreciation pattern. Due to the results of the regression model, Peles (1988) states that the true depreciation function is probably somewhere between the straight line and the declining balance method.[38]

An international comparison of the depreciation pattern of automobiles is given in Storchmann (2004). There, used-car prices of 54 different models and 30 different countries are analyzed from the period January 2001 to April 2001. Again, the one-hoss shay pattern, the straight-line pattern and the geometric pattern decay are distinguished and the best fit to one of these depreciation patterns are investigated. Storchmann (2004) shows that either the straight-line or the geometric depreciation pattern are applicable to explain the prices of automobiles. However, in most cases the geometric pattern decay achieves the best goodness of fit. Only for four out of 54 models the straight-line depreciation pattern performs best. Furthermore, comparing the depreciation pattern between developing (non-OECD countries) and developed countries (OECD countries), Storchmann (2004) finds that the depreciation rate is much higher for developed countries than for developing countries. As an explanation for the higher rate of depreciation in the

---

[37]See Ohta and Griliches (1976, p. 360 ff.).
[38]See Peles (1988, p. 49 ff.).

OECD countries, Storchmann (2004) states that the economic life of automobiles in poor countries is significantly longer than it is in wealthy countries.[39]

Summarizing, it can generally be said that by exponential depreciation pattern the best approximation of the automobile loss in value can be obtained. As shown in Table 3.3 this is approximated in most research paper by a geometric depreciation pattern (six studies), dummy variables for each year (seven studies) or higher order polynomials (three studies). In nine studies, the straight line depreciation pattern is chosen.

Table 3.3: **Number of publications categorized by their modeled depreciation pattern**

Depreciation pattern	#
Straight line	9
Geometric	6
Higher order polynomial	3
Year dummy	7

Moreover, a sensitivity of the depreciation pattern to external influences and different models and makes is evident. For this reason, in the following sections, the depreciation of cars is analyzed in more detail and other effects that influence the prices of automobiles are introduced.

3.2.2 Car-Specific Depreciation Factors

Whilst the previous section analyzes the depreciation pattern of automobiles over the time rather generally, Section 3.2.2 investigates the particular car-specific factors X_i and their effects on the depreciation rate of used cars. A general approach in the literature is a hedonic pricing model. This model is based on the assumption that the car price can be explained by its constituent characteristics and estimates of the contributory value of each characteristic can be obtained. Consequently, the total car price can be determined by the sum of the implicit prices of all individual components since each car can be defined

---

[39]See Storchmann (2004, p. 382 ff.).

as a bundle of different car characteristics. The prices of each individual attribute can be estimated from different specifications of the same product with varying characteristics of the specific component. To analyze the price effect due to different quality levels (e.g. number of kilometers, horsepower etc.) separately from mere price movements (due to e.g. make, color, etc.) a linear regression model with log-linear functional form as described by Equation 3.2 is often recommended in the literature (cf. Table 3.2).

Using the explained hedonic pricing approach, Ohta and Griliches (1976) analyze new-car and used-car prices for the U.S. automotive market. Their analyses are based on a data set of thirteen different domestic car makes from the years 1955 through 1971. They observe several factors regarding their effects on the prices of used cars. The variables of interest are classified into two different categories: for one thing physical factors (horsepower, weight, length) that directly affect the manufacturer cost function and for another thing performance factors that affect the utility function of the consumer. Examples for performance variables are acceleration, handling, steering, accommodation and fuel economy. Then, they perform regression analyses by using a semi-logarithmic functional form to investigate the effect of those characteristics on the car price. In a first step, Ohta and Griliches (1976) focus solely on the physical characteristics using two different approaches to evaluate their effect on car prices.

In their first approach, Ohta and Griliches (1976) assume a constant magnitude of the variables' price effect over the observation period 1961 till 1971. They define five physical variables that measure the engine power, the shipping weight, the length of the car and whether the car has a V8-engine or a hardtop (dummy variables). Additionally, dummy variables are defined for each year from 1961 through 1971, twelve car makes and the age of the car (two till six years old cars). The regression achieves a coefficient of determination of 92.6 percent. Statistically significant effects on the car prices can be verified for the engine power, shipping weight and the dummy variable that indicate whether the car has a V8-engine and a hardtop. The length of the car does not show any significant influence on the prices of cars.[40]

---

[40]See Ohta and Griliches (1976, p. 351 ff., p. 387 f.).

In their second approach, Ohta and Griliches (1976) divide the observation period into overlapping time intervals of two years to allow for varying regression coefficients over the time.[41] Hence, regression analyses were performed for two consecutive years. The same variables as in the first approach are used except for the dummy variables for the years 1961 through 1971. For all regression models, the R^2 is greater than 95%, which indicates a good explanation of the observed variance. Again, positive significant effects of the engine power, the V8-engine and hardtop dummy variables are detected, whereas no clear assertion about the effect of the shipping weight and the length of the car can be made. Depending on the considered time interval, for these two variables, significant positive price effects or negative price effects can be observed. This may be resulting from a high correlation between some of the models independent variables under consideration. Analyzing the effect of the car make in more detail, Ohta and Griliches (1976) find that high-priced makes have a significant price-increasing effect and low-priced makes a significant price decreasing effect. However, Ohta and Griliches (1976) declare that the make effect may result from unmeasured aspects of quality as they were not able to consider all relevant physical characteristics in their regression model.[42]

After their analyses of the effect of physical variables on the car prices, in the second step, Ohta and Griliches (1976) focus on performance variables. For this purpose, they include the following performance variables in their regression analyses: handling, steering, engine (smoothness and sound), engine power, automatic transmission, ride, accommodation, probable trade-in value, probable dollar depreciation and frequency of repair costs. All performance variables are derived from the results of road tests, ratings and frequency of repair records given in consumer reports and are transformed into a pre-defined arbitrary scale.[43] The variables measuring car age, the make of the car and the dummy variables of the year are still included in their model. Ohta and Griliches (1976) find that most performance variables do not show any significant effect on car prices. However, they demonstrate that performance variables appear to be useful in explaining car prices, even though the residual standard error is slightly smaller when using phys-

---

[41] Because of the odd year number, the first time interval consists of three years.

[42] See Ohta and Griliches (1976, p. 353 ff.).

[43] See Ohta and Griliches (1976, p. 368).

ical variables. The reason for the good explanatory power of the performance variables is that those variables that show a statistically and economically significant effect are highly correlated with either physical variables or the depreciation rate. In contrast, a high correlation to physical characteristics or the depreciation rate cannot be observed for non-significant performance variables.[44]

Summarizing, Ohta and Griliches (1976) show that physical variables describe used-car prices quite well. The R^2 of all their regressions is greater than 92%. Furthermore, their applied performance variables do not offer any additionally explanatory power because due to high correlation their effect is already covered by the physical characteristics.

An extension of the study of Ohta and Griliches (1976) can be found in Gordon (1990). Again, price effects in the U.S. automobile market are analyzed and only domestically produced cars are considered. The applied data set consists of one and two years old cars and take only four-door sedans into account. Gordon (1990) extends the observation period to the years 1947 through 1983 and uses more or less the same physical variables as Ohta and Griliches (1976) to perform semi-logarithmic regression analyses. Additionally to the variables used by Ohta and Griliches (1976), Gordon (1990) implements a variable that describes the level of trim, which is one for the most expensive trim and four for the cheapest trim. Another difference to Ohta and Griliches (1976) is the usage of four dummy variables for the engine types of his sample (4 cylinder, 6 cylinder, straight 8 or V-8). In the first step, 36 regression analyses were performed for intervals of two overlapping years and in the second step, five regression analyses for intervals of seven years.

The regression results for the first approach, which considers two successive years, show that, in most cases, the variables weight and brake horsepower have a positive effect on the car prices even though the results differ in their significance levels. The variable that measures the level of trim is always negative except for one interval. Hence, an expensive level of trim increases the used-car value and will be honored in the secondary market. The other variables do not show a clear effect. The R^2 of all these regressions is between 37.7% and 97.1%.

---

[44]See Ohta and Griliches (1976, p. 371).

The pooled regression results for the seven years periods confirm these results. The weight has a highly significant positive effect on the car prices and the age a highly significant negative effect. Again, the level of trim always lowers the used-car value. The regressions R^2 ranges from 78.7% to 90.4%.

To conclude, Gordon (1990) confirms the results of Ohta and Griliches (1976) and extends their study by the variable level of trim. Gordon (1990) finds a negative price effect for a decreasing trim level. Additionally, he can verify the results for a longer observation period of time.

A study by Dexheimer (2003) applies the hedonic pricing approach for the German used-car market. The observation period covers the years from 2000 to 2003. For each month, the number of observed used-car sales ranges between 20,000 - 25,000. Logarithmic regression analyses were used to estimate the effects of several car characteristics on the used-car prices. The analyzed variables are car age, relative mileage, logarithmic deflated original new-car price, dummy variables for 15 different makes and a time variable for the observation month. The relative mileage is defined as the driven kilometers per month of age. Regression equations were implemented for two following months. As an exemplary result, the regression table for the two-month interval August and September 2013 are listed. The regression results show a negative significant effect of the car age and the relative mileage. Dexheimer (2003) interprets the coefficient as follows: projected over a year the price effect of car age is equivalent to a yearly mean reduction in value of approximately 16%. The influence of mileage on the sales price is far smaller and reaches only approximately 0.1% per average annual mileage.[45] A positive significant price effect results for the logarithmic-deflated original new-car price. The coefficient of 0.9156 reveals that there is a close link between the sales price and the deflated original price. Furthermore, using Volkswagen as the base variable, Dexheimer (2003) finds significant effects of the car make. The regression's R^2 of 96% confirms the high explanatory power as seen in former studies. To sum up, former results indicating significant price effects of the car age and brand effects are transferable to the German used-car market, too.[46]

---

[45]See Dexheimer (2003, p. 7).
[46]See Dexheimer (2003, p. 3 ff.).

Another study that applies the hedonic regression model for explaining prices in the German second-hand car market was done by Kihm and Vance (2016). They employ a huge data set that contains more than 370,000 observations of new-car and used-car resale prices in 2008 and distinguish between nearly 300 models. Kihm and Vance (2016) implement semi-logarithmic regression equations that use the logarithmized resale prices as dependent variable. The independent variables used in their models are: age, mileage, speed, engine capacity, horse power, fuel consumption, retail price and dummy variables for the car model. Again, the car age and the driven mileage negatively affect the resale price. The same is true for the fuel consumption, whereas horse power, engine capacity and the retail price have a positive effect on the car prices. The results are highly statistically significant. Only for the variable speed, a significant effect cannot be verified. The dummy variables for the car model are mostly significant and differ in their sign and effect size (reference model VW Golf). Interestingly, in contrast to Dexheimer (2003), the coefficient of the variable retail price is greater than one (1.199). This confirms the hypothesis that increases in the retail price disproportionately increase the car's resale value. The results of Kihm and Vance (2016) suggest that a 10% higher retail price, increases the used-car resale price by roughly 12%. According to Kihm and Vance (2016), this can be explained by the car equipment because better-equipped cars keep more of their value as some attributes are must-have features for high resale values. The goodness-of-fit of the regressions ranges between a R^2 of 94% and 97%.[47]

Using data on two-year-old cars of the U.S. automobile market sold in 1977 and 1979, Goodman (1983) investigates how much money are consumers willing to pay for a more fuel-efficient car. Both oil shocks during the 1970s and the resulting increase of gasoline prices have led to the production of considerably more fuel-efficient cars than their pre-decessors. Goodman (1983) constructs a hedonic price model that incorporates the miles per gallon designation as an proxy for car's fuel-efficiency to measure consumers reactions to the increased gasoline prices.[48] The results of the logarithmic regression analysis confirm the prior findings regarding the relationship between the miles per gallon variable

---

[47]See Kihm and Vance (2016, p. 8 ff.).
[48]See Goodman (1983, p. 249 f.).

and used-car prices. Whilst the results for the two-year-old 1977 models do not provide plausible interrelations, the results for the two-year-old 1975 models show an economically and statistically significant relationship between the miles per gallon indicator and consumers' willingness to pay. As an approximation for consumers' willingness to pay for a more fuel-efficient car, the partial derivative of the regression equation to the miles per gallon variable is used. The results imply that a 1% increase in miles per gallon leads to an approximately 2% decrease of consumers' willingness to pay for a more fuel-efficient car.[49]

Only little research exists that analyze the residual value effects of alternative engines such as electric motors or hybrid vehicles. Gilmore and Lave (2013) analyze the difference of the residual value between conventional gasoline vehicles and vehicles that provide higher fuel economy such as turbocharged direct injection (TDI) diesel and hybridized electric gasoline (HEV). These more fuel efficient cars have higher manufacturing costs and sell at higher prices than the cars with conventional drive. Gilmore and Lave (2013) apply approximately 14,000 observations from used-vehicle auctions of the U.S. automobile market in the years 2008 and 2009 for paired alternative and conventional vehicles to compare the difference in resale prices. Using regression analysis they show that higher fuel-economic vehicles retain a higher proportion of their initial purchase price than conventional vehicles. Furthermore, the ratio of the resale value to the initial price increases at higher fuel prices. As an explanation for this price premium, Gilmore and Lave (2013) declare that the discounted expected future fuel savings will be reflected in the pricing process of rational consumers.[50]

A different result can be found in the study of Majid and Russell (2015). This study compares the depreciation pattern of hybrid drives and conventional engines. For this purpose, investigating the U.S. car market, they employ a data set of eleven different models of cars manufactured by five different car manufacturers from the period June 2004 to September 2011. The car models can be categorized into conventionally driven cars, hybrid vehicles that are extensions of a previous brand and stand-alone hybrid vehicle

---

[49]See Goodman (1983, p. 258 ff.).
[50]See Gilmore and Lave (2013, p. 200).

brands. Using the proportion of the original value that remains at the sales date as the dependent variable, multiple regression analyses are applied. Besides dummy variables for the calendar year, market-specific and model-specific characteristics are implemented as explanatory variables. Market-specific variables are the average gas price and the total number of sold hybrid vehicles as a proportion of total vehicles sold. Model-specific variables are the logarithmized original car price, car age, the amount of advertising expenditure for each model, model reputation and dummy variables indicating a hybrid drive and whether this belongs to a hybrid brand extension. Majid and Russell (2015) find that hybrid technology has a significant negative impact on the value retained over time. Depending on the car model, the residual value effect ranges from five to eleven percentage points. Furthermore, their results imply that stand-alone hybrid vehicles, which are those cars without a non-hybrid alternative, retain more value over time than brand extension hybrid vehicles. Depending on the model, Majid and Russell (2015) detect significantly negative price effects for brand extension hybrid vehicles of eight and ten percentage points compared to the price of stand-alone hybrid vehicles. Furthermore, their third result shows that after the market introduction of an improved technology such as a fully electric engine, hybrid vehicles that are extensions of a previous brand lose greater value than stand-alone hybrid vehicle brands.

Automobile brand effects on the prices of used cars are subject of the study by Betts and Taran (2004). Specifically, Betts and Taran (2004) analyze a 'brand halo' effect, which means that the perceptions of a brand's overall attributes affect pricing beyond the effect of the specific qualities of a particular product within the brand.[51] The reliability of the car is a decisive factor in consumers' purchase decision. As an individual vehicle's reliability may not be clear at the moment of purchase, consumers rely on the car's reliability history. Based on available reports about the number of repairs by owners of such a model, a reliability scale is created for all car models and makes. Betts and Taran (2004) observe 17 different car brands of the U.S. automobile market during the years 1993 to 1999. According to the results of their regression analyses, they show that used-car prices are positively affected by both the reliability of a particular car model

---

[51]See Betts and Taran (2004, p. 1).

and the reliability associated with a brand overall. This means that beyond the effect of
the reliability history of a specific model the reliability associated with the brand has a
significant price effect.[52]

Another relevant factor for the valuation of a used car, is the car's amount of additional equipment. As already pointed out in Gordon (1990) the level of a car's trim and
its supplementary equipment can significantly affect automobile prices.[53] This can be
considered by adjusting the car prices in a so-call 'stripping' process and including variables for the trim level. However, knowing which additional equipment positively affects
the second-hand market price of a car, can be a decisive factor in consumers' purchase
decision.

The study of Prieto et al. (2015) focuses on the seller side and investigates price effects
resulting from car's deviations of the expected reliability, which is measured by the average driven kilometers per year. For this purpose, a hedonic price measurement is applied,
which considers additional equipments. The associated regression model is based on a
semi-logarithmic functional form. Their data set contains 1,735 advertisements of used
cars on Internet platforms during the three month time period January to March 2012.
The data set covers the four most popular and requested car segments. As explanatory
variables Prieto et al. (2015) incorporate car age, engine power, driven kilometers and
dummy variables for fuel type, car classification, sales region, body paintwork and the additional equipment. The additional equipment can be classified into dummy variables for
cruise control, anti-lock braking system, air conditioning system, navigation system and
metallic paintwork. The coefficients of the regression confirm the findings of the previous
studies regarding variables such as car age, engine power and driven kilometers. However,
some new results can be derived for the additional equipment and the color. Colors such
as white, red, green have a significantly negative effect on the used-car prices, whereas
the color black significantly increase the car's resale value. For optional equipment, a
price increasing impact can only be verified for cruise control, air conditioning system
and metallic paintwork. The other investigated additional equipments do not show any

---

[52]See Betts and Taran (2004, p. 7 ff.).
[53]See Gordon (1990, p. 340 ff.).

significant effect. To sum up, to increase the car's resale value, consumers should not choose exotic colors and have in mind which additional equipment positively affects the car's residual value.

Summarizing, this section deals with the identification of car-specific characteristics that influence cars' residual values. Across markets, the car age, mileage and the fuel consumption can be identified as residual value-reducing factors in particular. In contrast, the original price and the engine power positively affects the prices in the secondary market. The car brand significantly affects the prices of cars: cars that belong to a brand associated with high reliability can be resold for higher prices than cars belonging to brands associated with a low reliability level. Hybrid drives depreciate at a faster rate than automobiles with conventional drive. However, consumers can increase the resale value of their automobiles by the choice of their car's supplementary equipment and technical features. Table 3.4 summarizes the findings regarding relevant car-specific determinants that influence the prices of used vehicles. As expected car age, mileage, make, horsepower and the engine type are the most considered influencing factors of car prices in the secondary market.

Table 3.4: **Number of Publications Categorized by Car-Specific Variables**

variables	#	variables	#	variables	#
Age	23	Model	6	Segment/Size	3
Make/Brand	11	Weight	5	Other performance variables	3
Mileage	10	Number of cylinders	5	Length	2
Horsepower	9	Miles per gallon	4	Number of doors	2
Body type	8	Fuel economy	4	Safety	1
Engine type	8	Level of attributes/Extras	4	Number of seats	1
Transmission	7	(Top) speed	4	Color	1
Original car price	7	Reputation/Reliability	4		

3.2.3 Time-Dependent Depreciation Factors

Beside the identification of the influence of physical and performance variables, several studies focus on the analysis of macro-economic conditions and their effect on the prices in the second-hand car market. Used-car prices can be affected by changes in the economic and legal framework conditions and a changed customer behavior particularly with regard to their perception of the market activities and developments such as, for example, the development of gasoline prices or the gross domestic product (GDP). Hence, the focus of this approach and the following section is to identify the impact of the added time-dependent variable of interest.

Following their study of the year 1976, Ohta and Griliches (1986) extend their used hedonic regression model to test the influence of increasing gasoline costs on used-car prices. In their analysis, they focus on the impact of the oil crisis in the years 1973 and 1979 on the U.S. automobile market. It is investigated how consumers' quality perception changed due to increasing gasoline prices as a consequence of the crises. For this purpose, Ohta and Griliches (1986) test whether an additional term that capture the changes in the gasoline prices results in a stabilization of the physical variables over the course of time. In the case of neglected gasoline prices, their results reveal strong variations in the coefficients of the physical characteristics over time. However, by considering an additional term for gasoline costs, Ohta and Griliches (1986) show that the coefficients of the remaining characteristics are much more stable over time. Hence, they conclude that changes in consumers' valuation of physical car characteristics are a result of changing gasoline prices.[54]

Considering consumers' expectation about future gasoline prices and constructing hedonic used-car price indexes, Ohta (1987) even extends these findings. Again, this study takes into account the oil crises of the years 1973 and 1979. Based on the basic hedonic price index of Ohta and Griliches (1986) that focuses on physical characteristics, Ohta (1987) constructs three hedonic price index models under different assumptions about consumers' expectations about future gasoline prices. For the first index, the gasoline

---

[54]See Ohta and Griliches (1986, p. 193 ff.).

prices are assumed to be constant at the present level over time. In the second approach, the assumption is made that consumers expect constant gasoline prices at the present level over the remaining lifetime of the car, whereas the third index assumes that consumers expect increasing gasoline prices as they extrapolate some fraction of high gasoline price rises into the future.[55] Whereas the first index was estimated for all of the periods 1970-1983, regressions for the second and the third index only covers the period before, during and after the oil crises of 1973 and 1979. Analyzing the different proportional rate of change for those indexes, Ohta (1987) finds that consumers' expectations about future gasoline prices significantly affect prices in the secondary market. For both years of the oil crisis the proportional rate of change of the second and third index is significantly higher than the proportional rate of change of the first index. Thus, consumers anticipate that gasoline costs stay at the current high level or even increase in the future. The proportional rate of change of the third index shows the highest effect, even though significant for the second oil crisis only. In this case, consumers feared a rise in prices in the future. In total, Ohta (1987) finds a significant effect of consumers' expectations of gasoline prices, which results in large variations in used-car price indexes.[56]

Another study that examines the impact of changes in gasoline price expectations on the market values of used automobiles is the paper of Kahn (1986). Using market data of American used automobiles that covers the years 1972 through 1981, Kahn (1986) investigates how the prices of used cars of different fuel-efficiency classes react to gasoline price fluctuations. Consumers' expectations about future gasoline prices are modeled in two alternative ways. The first assumes that consumers expect stable gasoline prices and uses the current real price as the best predictor for future gasoline prices. The second approach models future gasoline prices by means of an appropriate autoregressive integrated moving average (ARIMA) process. The used gasoline prices of the years 1962 to 1981 indicate that the best forecast of the rate of change for more than one period into the future is just the mean over the sample period.[57] The empirical results imply that changes

---

[55]See Ohta (1987, p. 521 ff.).
[56]See Ohta (1987, p. 523 ff.).
[57]See Kahn (1986, p. 330 ff.).

in gasoline prices cause relative price adjustments across automobiles with different levels
of fuel efficiency in proportion to the differences in their rates of fuel consumption.

Storchmann (2004) analyzes the effects of market factors on the prices in the used-car
market for different countries, which are categorized into OECD and non-OECD countries. Thereby, he focuses on gasoline prices and per-capita private consumption as an
approximation for income. Private consumption is used because of the closer link to private automobiles than the GDP does. Further variables indicate the list price of a new
car and whether the car is a pick-up truck or not. The depreciation rate is used as the
dependent variable in the regression model. In the cross-sectional analysis of international used-car prices from 30 countries and 54 models of 2001, Storchmann (2004) finds
that private consumption has a positive effect on the depreciation rate and the new-car
list price as well as the dummy variable for a pick-up truck a negative price effect. The
respective coefficients are statistically significant on the 1% level for the whole sample.
A separate regression analysis for the OECD and non-OECD countries shows that private consumption is positive and significant for both samples. Hence, income increases
depreciation rates in developed as well as emerging markets. In contrast, the gasoline
price is only positive and statistically significant for the OECD countries. For non-OECD
countries only the pick-up truck dummy variable has a highly significant negative effect
on the used-car depreciation. As an explanation for the higher depreciation due to increasing gasoline prices, Storchmann (2004) states that consumers are willing to pay for
a more fuel-efficient car as a substitution of their contemporary old car. This results in a
decreasing demand for used cars and in an accelerated depreciation.[58]

The study of Busse et al. (2009) investigates how gasoline prices affect prices of cars in
the second-hand car market, which have different levels of fuel efficiency. Their data set
contains automobile transactions in the U.S. car market from 1999 to 2008. Depending
on the car's fuel-efficiency measured in miles per gallon, it is assigned to one of four
groups ranging from less to high fuel-efficient. In a second step, another classification is
done that considers the car segments. The price effect on used cars due to changes in

---

[58]See Storchmann (2004, p. 399 ff.).

gasoline prices is estimated via regression analysis. Busse et al. (2009) find a very large effect of gasoline price changes on used-car prices. An increase in gasoline prices leads to decreasing prices, which are the most for the least fuel-efficient cars (small miles per gallon designation) and to rising prices which are the most for the most fuel-efficient cars (high miles per gallon designation). Similar results are found for the categorization into car segments. Especially for the SUV segment, strong price movements are estimated by changing gasoline prices.[59]

These results of the price effects of increasing gasoline prices are confirmed by a recent study of Busse et al. (2013a), which uses the same data set about automobile transactions as Busse et al. (2009). For each transaction, car-specific information about the purchased vehicle and the price paid for the car are observable as well as (census-based) demographic information about the customer. Information about the exact vehicle purchased contains the car age, mileage, model year, engine power, number of cylinder, gear type and fuel-efficiency. Demographic information describes the income, house value and ownership, household size, vehicles per household, education, occupation, average travel time to work, English proficiency and the buyer's race. Additionally, gasoline prices are considered by taken regional differences into account. Using multiple regression analysis, Busse et al. (2013a) find significant effects of gasoline prices on short-run equilibrium prices of cars of different fuel economies. For new cars, the effect of an $1 increase in the price of gasoline is associated with an increase of $104 in the average price of the highest fuel economy cars and a price decrease of $250 in the average price of the lowest fuel economy cars. For used cars, the result shows the same effect; however, the estimated relative price difference between the highest and lowest fuel-efficient cars is much greater and increases to $1,945. Compared to their earlier study, the price decrease of low fuel-efficient cars and the price increase of high fuel-efficient cars are much stronger.[60]

Using over 35,000 used-car transaction of the U.S. car market during the period 1999 to 2009, Jacobsen and Van Benthem (2015) find similar results as Busse et al. (2013a). Controlling for horsepower, weight and the original suggested retail price, their regression

---

[59]See Busse et al. (2009, p. 25 ff.).
[60]See Busse et al. (2013a, p. 232 ff.).

results show that a $1 increase in the gasoline price implies a $1,401 increase in the average used-car prices in the most efficient quartile relative to the least efficient. Dividing the data set into age categories and repeating the regression analysis reveals that this effect decreases by age and range between $2,121 among the newest used cars to less than $800 among used vehicles ten years and older. As the vehicles of the newest car category are the closest comparison to the sample of Busse et al. (2013a), the results of Jacobsen and Van Benthem (2015) confirm the earlier findings of Busse et al. (2013a) very accurate.

Purohit (1992) explores the relationship between the markets for new and used automobiles. In the focus of this study is the effect of changes incorporated in new versions of automobiles on prices of older versions in the secondary market. Such changes can be, for example, variations of existing models or the introduction of new models. Moreover, the price effects in the used-car market resulting from model elimination are analyzed. In the study, Purohit (1992) uses a data set of 57 car models and nine different U.S. makes covering the period from 1975 to 1985. Cars older than five years or newer than one year are excluded from the analysis. To measure the effect of changes in the primary market on the prices in the second-hand market eight semi-logarithmic regression analyses that use the logarithmic car price as dependent variable were conducted. The regression analyses have been carried out separately for seven car segments. Characteristics of automobiles measured by the explanatory variables are categorized broadly as quantitative and perceptual attributes. Quantitative attributes are those characteristics that are easily measurable such as horsepower, whereas the perceptual attributes on which Purohit (1992) focuses is styling. Four levels to categorize the degree of styling changes from the previous model year are used. Smaller changes are for example a grille change or a tail-lamp change. In contrast, a sheetmetal change, a larger platform or downsizing are categorized as large changes. Besides a variable measuring the percentage changes in horsepower, a variable for the list price and car age are implemented. Additionally, dummy variables for the make, the year and the level of the perceptual attributes' changes are introduced. Moreover, another dummy variable indicates whether there is a downsizing in model m's sister car at time t. Using regression analyses, Purohit (1992) shows that second-hand market prices respond to changes in the primary market: for three of seven car segments, a significant negative effect can be verified for changes in horsepower compared to the previous model. Styling changes, however, can have significant positive or negative price effects on used cars depending whether the styling change of the new car is viewed positively or not. Hence, it is not clear from the outset whether a change in the styling will be valuated positively. Purohit (1992) shows that certain major model changes have an effect not only on older cars of the same model but also on sister models made by the same manufacturer. Furthermore, positive second-hand price effects can be a result from a discontinuation of certain models from the product line. The regression R^2 ranges between 0.68 and 0.92.

As seen in the studies by Ohta and Griliches (1976) and Betts and Taran (2004) the quality of a car or its reputation, which was approximated by the car brand, is one major factor in consumers' purchase decision. Another indicator for a car's quality was investigated by Hartman (1987). In this study, the effect of product recalls on the used-car prices is analyzed. Using U.S. automobile market data of all domestic and imported models of the year 1980, which were sold in the years 1981 to 1985, Hartman (1987) focuses on how to measure and to take into account the new information regarding product recalls, which were made for reasons of safety. By applying the hedonic methodology together with logarithmic regression equations that consider physical car characteristics and dummy variables for the age and the car segment, the price effect due to product recalls is investigated. In the first step, this is done for product recalls for each car segment and in a second step for the reason of recall (engine problems, brake defect, others). Hartman (1987) finds evidence that used-car prices decline as a reason of manufacturer recalls of the automobile due to defective safety equipment. It is shown that the intensity of the price effect differs between segments, the defect type and the number of affected cars. For example, automobile recalls due to engine problems lead to higher price declines than recalls due to brake defects. Contagion effects for other models of the car manufacturer who has announced the product recall are not identified by Hartman (1987).

Another paper dealing with a similar topic was written by Hammond (2013). He investigates how consumers response to large-scale product recalls that are caused by safety problems. In the empirical analysis, the used-car prices of Toyota Motors vehicles are compared to the used-car prices of other domestic and foreign manufacturers in the U.S. secondary car market. As a consequence of safety deficiencies more than nine million Toyota Motors vehicles were recalled in the years 2009-2010. The study by Hammond (2013) aims to measure the treatment effect of a recall on prices of Toyota vehicles in the second-hand car market. By using panel data, this is done by a difference-in-difference estimation approach that allows for time-varying treatment effects and serial correlation. The treatment group and the control group are defined by Toyota vehicles and the vehicles of the other car manufacturers, respectively. Hammond (2013) finds that the large-scale product recall by Toyota does not have a statistically significant price effect on automobiles which were produced by the affected car manufacturer. Although some short-term and quantitatively small negative price effects are observable, they are not distinguishable from zero. However, comparing price declines due to a product recall by Audi in the 1980s, Hammond (2013) concludes that the extent of the price effect of product recalls in the used-car market depends more on the manufacturer's established reputation in the car market than on the reputation for producing high-quality automobiles.[61]

During the last decades, governmental regulatory interventions resulted in an intensification of emission and safety requirements, especially for new cars. Considering the period from 1972 to 1991 and the American used-car market, Dunham (1997) analyzes whether these regulatory changes are valued by consumers. This is done by a linear regression analysis, where vehicle's depreciation rate is used as the dependent variable. As control variables, Dunham (1997) implements dummy variables for the age, year and the manufacturer and dummy variables to measure the change in cost for new vehicles due to changes in emission control regulations and safety regulations. The regression results reveal that consumers evaluate differently these two regulation types. Changes in emission regulations increase the prices of used vehicles, whereas changes in safety regulations result in a price decline of cars in the secondary market. The effects are explained by the competitiveness of the new-car market and the used-car market. Price increases of used vehicles due to changes in emission regulations are a result of an increasing demand for

---

[61]During that time Audi starts entering the American car market and had only a small market share.

less expensive and older cars, whereas consumer's demand for expensive new cars decline. As new and used cars are substitutes and because of the price increase of new cars due to new emission standards, consumers change their decision to buy a new car and decide to buy a used car instead. Finally, this higher demand leads to an price increase of used vehicles. The second effect resulting from new safety regulations is explained by consumers' percipience of the higher safety standard. The contemporary safety level of used cars is perceived as insufficient. Hence, consumers decide buying new cars instead of used cars. To sum up, consumers perceive emission regulations rather as a fee without benefit, whereas they are willing to pay for higher safety standards.[62]

Besides several car-specific factors, Prado (2009) also implements market factors in his hedonic model to estimate the distribution of resale prices. Using sales data of a major leasing company from 2004 to 2008, the model is applied to four European markets, France, Germany, Spain and Great Britain, to quantify the hedonic price. For the hedonic price measurement, the linear regression model is used. To control for differences in market conditions, the regression model is applied for all four countries separately. The real resale price is used as the dependent variable. The explanatory variables of the regression models can be categorized into four groups: the first group describes the vehicle's wear and tear during the vehicle's life and controls for the age, distance traveled and the miles per month. The second group considers manufacturer-specific effects, which are modeled by dummy variables for the brand and by a cubicle variable of the list price taking into account that a high initial price increases devaluation. Variables describing the developments in the different markets constitute the third group. Those are approximated by the diesel pump price, the industrial production index and the quarter sale date. Physical characteristics of the vehicle are considered by the last group of variables. Information about the average fuel consumption, body type, number of seats, engine power, number of cylinders, automatic transmission and the number of doors are given, which are slightly different from one country to another. For instance, for the German market, information

---

[62]See Dunham (1997, p. 584 ff.).

about the numbers of cylinders, automatic transmission and the number of seats are not available.[63]

The regression analyses show an explained variance in the range of 75% (for the German market) to 81% (for the French market). Almost all variables have a significant effect on the 1% level and a significant economic value. The physical characteristics adding quality to the car such as engine power and number of seats have an price-increasing effect. A higher fuel consumption reduce the vehicle's resale value. The industrial production, which is used as an approximation of budget variation has a positive sign. On the contrary, the price of fuel has a negative effect because it is an additional cost of the driving activity. As stated by Dunham (1997), an increase in fuel prices leads to an reduced demand for used cars because consumers decide to purchase a more fuel-efficient new car. Variables of the first category, which are correlated to obsolescence and wear have a price-reducing effect on the used cars. The dummy variables for the sales quarter show a slightly seasonal effect in all markets. Vehicles that were produced by German car manufacturers show positive make effects, which are verified for all countries. This can be explained by a high reputation of German cars due to their recognized quality.[64]

In a next step, Prado (2009) focuses on the models Ford Focus and Audi A4, which are present in all four countries, to compare the four markets with regard to the vehicles' resale price distribution and the amount of information available from historical sales. On the one hand, markets with higher valuation of used vehicles should reveal better opportunities but on the other hand markets with a higher volatility of resale prices indicate a higher risk due to the increased uncertainty of the resale price. The results show that there exists a high volatility in all countries. On average, the resale price in Germany is the highest; however, the German market has the highest standard deviation, which implies a higher risk of value losses. Analyzing the resale price distribution through age and mileage gives insights into the depreciation pattern of different countries. The findings

---

[63] See Prado (2009, p. 13).
[64] See Prado (2009, p. 15 ff.).

of Prado (2009) show that hedonic valuations are significantly different by country, which implies that European markets are not homogeneous.[65]

Contrary to the former studies, Nau (2012) keeps the car age as constant over time by collecting average used-car prices for different car models. The prices of the used vehicles were adjusted for mileage resulting in a homogenous sample over time. The advantage of using average prices of different car models that do not differ over time is that variations in prices are only a result of temporal developments in the used-car market, which is in the focus of this study. For the analysis, Nau (2012) uses a data set consisting of 17 different car models of the German automobile market during the observation period from June 1992 to December 2008. The car models under consideration are selected from the highest volume vehicles of the five largest car segments, which are for at least 22 years available in the German automobile market. The age of the cars is set to 36 month.[66]

To describe movements in the residual values, explanatory variables were defined, which can be categorized into three groups: one group that consists of variables specifying the economy, one for variables characterizing the new-car market and the used-car market and one group for variables describing a specific car model. Developments in the economy are modeled by the quarterly GDP, quarterly private consumption spendings, monthly change in percentage of the unemployment rate and rates of the Euro interbank offered rate (EURIBOR) three-month fund for the period from January 1999 to December 2008 and the rates of the Frankfurt interbank offered rate (FIBOR) three-month fund before 1999. Developments in the new-car market and used-car market are modeled by the number of monthly new-car registrations, the number of cars that change ownership within one month and the petrol price. The last category consists of variables that specify model characteristics. These are the number of months the car model has already been available in the used-car market, dummy variables indicating a model cycle, a dummy variable indicating whether a new model is launched or not and a dummy variable that equals one if a facelift is launched in the used-car market or zero if otherwise.[67]

---

[65]See Prado (2009, p. 16 f.).
[66]See Nau (2012, p. 61 f.).
[67]See Nau (2012, p. 64 ff.).

Furthermore, Nau (2012) defines the used-car retail price divided by the latest manufacturer's retail price as the dependent variable to ensure comparability of the residual
values of the same car over time and between different car models. A regression analysis is performed for each car model. In the regression analysis, Nau (2012) includes a
lagged dependent variable to overcome the shortcoming of a serial correlation of the error term. In the case that the serial correlation of the error term remains, an ARMAX
time series regression model is applied, which is a linear regression model that uses an
autoregressive-moving-average (ARMA) model for the error terms. The results show that
mainly the car-model-specific factors have a significant effect on residual values. The number of months a car is available in the used-car market negatively affects the used-car
value. The effect is highly significant for the majority of the investigated car models.
The launch of new car models and a facelift also have a significant effect on the retail
prices. However, the direction of the effect depends on the car model. Moreover, Nau
(2012) finds that the developments in the new-car market and used-car market rather
influence residual values than the developments described by the variables characterizing
the overall economy. For many car models significant positive effects are estimated for the
number of new registrations and the number of changed ownerships. As an explanation
for this effect, Nau (2012) states that an increased demand for cars results into higher
residual values. The variable measuring the petrol price is only significantly negative for
three car models. For the other variables indicating the economic development over the
time, there does not exist a particular underlying factor, which is significant throughout
(almost) all car models. This is explained by the meaning of the car for most households.
The ownership of a car is essential to ensure households' mobility and therefore does a
change in the economic and financial environment not influence households' decision to
purchase a car substantially. [68]

Although the variables specifying the economic developments do not show a clear
significant price effect, some characteristics can be derived from the results for a certain
car segment. For instance, the GDP and the private consumption significantly affect
the residual values of small cars. These cars seem to be more receptive for changes in

---

[68]See Nau (2012, p. 71 ff.).

households' financial situation than cars of the upper segments. Moreover, significant positive effects can be derived from an increasing unemployment. Again, this increase is only significant for the small car segments. According to Nau (2012), due to a higher unemployment people are forced to buy either a used car or a car of a lower segment. In contrast to the price sensitivity of cars from the small car segments to the economic developments, cars of the upper segments are not affected by changes in the economy. Nau (2012) states that consumers of the upper segment cars are less sensitive to change in the economical situation as they consider their cars as a status symbol. Analyzing the results with regard to the brand reveals that a car's popularity and reliability has a significant effect on its residual value.[69]

Summarizing, it was shown, that the price of an used automobile not only depends on the wear of the physical characteristics but on the developments in the automobile market. Relevant factors are gasoline prices and the car's fuel-efficiency. In addition, there is a strong interaction between the primary and secondary market. Changes in the market for new cars such as the introduction of a new car model or a facelift can significantly affect the prices in the used-car market. Governmental interaction can also result in price changes of used automobiles due to changes in demand and supply. Furthermore, the reliability of a car indicated by product recalls can affect the secondary-market prices. Only little evidences for price effects on used cars are found for macro-economic factors. The small car segments are more sensitive to economic developments because for cars of these segments, there are significant effects to changes in the GDP, private consumption and the unemployment rate detectable. Hence, a separate analysis for different car segments is recommendable when assessing residual values.

Table 3.5 illustrates the research focus regarding time-dependent factors. Gasoline prices are considered by most studies. However, for macro-economic effects, a clear factor that is considered as important in many studies is not detectable. Instead, dummy variables describing the time of resale are often implemented in the regression analyses to control for the effects of the developments in the overall markets.

---

[69]See Nau (2012, p. 84).

Table 3.5: **Number of Publications Categorized by Time-Specific Variables**

Variables	#	Variables	#
Gasoline prices	9	GDP	1
Time dummy variables	8	Industrial Production Index	1
Income	5	Private Consumption Index	1
Model launch/change	3	Euribor	1
Facelift/styling change	2	Number of new car registrations	1
Product recall	2	Number of changes of ownership	1
Other demographic variables	2	Model cycle	1
Advertising expenditures	1	Number of sold hybrid vehicles	1

3.2.4 Other Residual Value Influencing Factors

Another stream in the literature considers the effect of the Internet and the corresponding information processing on the prices of used automobiles. Although some of these studies focus on the prices of new cars, these results may be of high relevance for prices in the secondary market, too. This is reasoned by the interdependencies between the primary and secondary car market as seen in Section 3.2.3

Morton et al. (2001) investigate the effect of Internet car referral services on the prices of dealer-offered automobiles. Internet referral services are sites related to new-car purchases that provide information about individual cars, current market conditions and invoice pricing. Additionally, Internet referral sites are in close contractual relations with dealers and pass on customers' purchase requests to their dealer network. Using a data set of approximately 187,000 vehicle purchases in California during the period from January 1999 to February 2000 and a regression analysis, Morton et al. (2001) find that customers of an Internet car referral service pay on average 2% less for their car. This is explained by better price conditions resulting from the dealers affiliated to an online service; however, the lower prices are mainly a result of information provision and bargaining by the Internet car referral service as well as cost efficiencies.[70]

By using matched survey and transaction data on 1,500 car purchases in California, Zettelmeyer et al. (2006) confirm that the Internet reduces automobile prices. Their

---

[70]See Morton et al. (2001, p. 501 ff.).

regression results reveal two reasons: first, customers that use the Internet are better informed about dealers invoice prices. Second, Internet car referral services help customers to obtain lower prices. The overall price effect of informed customers that uses an online referral service is -1.5%. However, the effect differs by consumer type. Customers who dislike bargaining and have collected information about the car of interest pay on average 1.5% less than customers without these information. Consumers who like to bargain do not benefit from collected information about the car they eventually purchase.[71]

Andrews and Benzing (2007) investigate determinants of prices in an eBay used-car auction market. Using a data set of 437 observations, they focus on the influence of auction, seller and product factors on the price premium. In their regression analysis, they find significant effects on the bid price premium in used-car auctions for a clear auction title, the seller reputation and when the auction ended. On average, used cars which were offered for sale by a professional dealer and that have a clear auction title can be sold with significant positive price premiums.[72]

Engers et al. (2009) investigate whether the net benefits from owning a vehicle, approximated by annual miles driven, explain the price declines observed over a vehicle's life cycle. In the first step, Engers et al. (2009) model households' decision on how much to drive each of its automobiles. For this purpose, certain factors are considered that affect households' yearly driven mileage or rather the net benefit that is assigned to each of the household's vehicles. Those determinants taken into account are family income, location characteristics such as an urban area and the number of drivers in a household classified by age, gender and work status. Additionally, Engers et al. (2009) observe each vehicle owned by the household and have information about its age, brand and annual miles driven.[73] To estimate households decision regarding each car's annual driven miles, two models are estimated for several car makes to describe the interrelation between the annual miles and households' characteristics: a basic OLS model that assumes a linear relationship between household's characteristics and the mileage per year and a struc-

---

[71]See Zettelmeyer et al. (2006, p. 179).
[72]See Andrews and Benzing (2007, p. 55 f.).
[73]See Engers et al. (2009, p. 25 f.).

tural model. The second approach models this relationship non-linearly. Additionally, it takes into account the portfolio of cars owned by a household, which is characterized by the number and the age distribution of vehicles, to consider the household's decision to drive a car on a certain trip. Using observations for the U.S. car market of the year 1995, their empirical results indicate that the non-linear approach better explains the annual driven miles than the OLS estimates. Engers et al. (2009) show that the income and the number of drivers in a household positively affect the miles per year, whereas the annual miles driven decrease in the age of the car.[74]

In the second step, analyzing used-car prices for the years 1986-2000, Engers et al. (2009) find that variation in household's annual miles across brands explains observed price declines. Again, the structural approach performs better in explaining the variation in price declines across brands than the OLS model. Furthermore, their results imply that the effect of vehicles' age on annual miles and consequently on the decline of used-car prices can be classified by three components: a pure aging effect, an effect stemming from the household's car portfolio and an effect depending on the household's demographic characteristics. Hence, this study provides evidence that the decline in used-car prices cannot only be explained by the car's aging. Other determinants such as the household's income and the car portfolio that affect the usage of household's cars over the life cycle have to taken into account.[75]

To sum up, there are other factors than physical characteristics and the development of the markets that can significantly affect the prices in the second-hand automobile market. The presented studies show that the final used-car prices depend on the consumer type. Consumer's information level and the usage of online services can significantly reduce the purchase price. Furthermore, household-specific determinants such as income and demographic factors are of high relevance.

---

[74]See Engers et al. (2009, p. 12 ff.).
[75]See Engers et al. (2009, p. 19 ff.).

3.3 Interim results

The identification of determinants that influence the prices of used cars is attracting great interest among buyers and sellers of used automobiles. Not only households are interested in a correct valuation of the used car they want to sell or buy, but rather leasing companies and financial institutions that are exposed to a high concentration of the residual value risk. Leasing companies have to sell the leased vehicle in the secondary market after the end of the lease term. However, the value of the leased vehicle can be lower than the predefined contractual residual value at the start of the leasing agreement. Credit institutes often use the borrowers' cars as additional securities for their loans. Hence, an adequate assessment of all the relevant residual value influencing factors is essential for a reasonable forecast of the future used-car value.

The literature shows that there are many different factors that influence the used-car prices. Generally, an exponential depreciation pattern over time is observable. A significant impact on the automobiles' secondary-market prices are verifiable for physical and car-specific characteristics. In particular, the car age, mileage and the fuel consumption can be identified as residual value-reducing factors, whereas the brand's reliability and supplementary equipment can increase the resale value. In addition, the developments in the car markets are important to explain changes in the secondary-market prices over time. Relevant factors are gasoline prices and the car's fuel-efficiency. Furthermore, there is a strong interaction of the primary and secondary market so that changes in the primary market such as the introduction of new car models or variants directly affects the prices in the used-car market. Changes in the macroeconomic environment, measured by the GDP, private consumption and the unemployment rate only affect the prices of the small car segments.

From the literature review implication for future research can be drawn. Despite the identification of lots of significant determinants that influence the prices of used cars, their may still exist other relevant factors that have to be analyzed. For instance, the results of the literature review imply that automobile prices depend on consumers' information provision. However, people are limited in their information processing and do not always behave rational. Hence, this could result in price discrepancies, which cannot be explained by other observable determinants. Chapter 4 addresses this limited information processing and investigates how the pricing process for used cars is affected by individuals who exhibit a heuristic known as anchoring when they incorporate the age of a car into their pricing decision.

In addition, as seen in the literature review, governmental interaction can also result in price changes of used automobiles due to changes in demand and supply. In the last decades, scrappage schemes are frequently used political measures to stimulate the economic situation and to reduce the emission of greenhouse gases. Analyzing the price effects of accelerated vehicle retirement programs are therefore of high relevance. Furthermore, as most studies focus on the U.S. automobile market, there is a need for future research on other important automobile markets. Table 3.6 illustrates the research focus on the U.S. used-car market. 26 out of 33 research papers employ a data set of used-car sales in the United States.

Table 3.6: **Number of Publications Categorized by Car Markets**

Country	Thereof	#	#
North America	USA	27	26
Europe	Germany/France	8	6/3
South America		1	
Central America		1	
Asia		1	
Australia		1	
Africa		1	

Against this background, in Chapter 5, the price effect of demand and supply shocks on used automobiles due to the German srappage scheme of 2009 is analyzed.

4 Anchoring and Price Anomalies

4.1 Fundamentals and Research Questions

The literature review of Chapter 3 shows that physical characteristics, brand effects and the developments in the primary and secondary car market significantly affect the prices of used-cars. Many of the presented studies have the presence of a perfect market with rational individuals and transparent information available to all market participants in common, which implies that the prices of goods fully reflect all available information about both the product and the market (Malkiel and Fama, 1970). However, economists agree that individuals have limited cognitive abilities to incorporate the masses of information that are observable in the market into their price assessments (Simon, 1955; Grossman and Stiglitz, 1980). The literature emphasizes that individuals rely on simple heuristics and only consider a subset of information in their decision making.[76] As a result, prices of goods differ from their rational expectations.

Against this background, in this chapter, the focus of the analyses are the following research questions:

- What is the effect of individuals' heuristic information processing on the prices of used cars?
- Can professional sellers exploit individuals' heuristic car evaluation?
- Does an increase in individuals' cognitive abilities reduce the size of the price effect of individuals' heuristic information processing?

---

[76]See Gilovich et al. (2002) for an overview.

The established empirical analysis, the theoretical conception and the findings of this chapter are based on a paper written by Gürtler and Gutknecht (2016).

The effects of heuristic information processing on prices in the used-car market are studied. Thereby, it is strived to explain, how the pricing process for used cars is affected by individuals who exhibit a heuristic known as anchoring when they incorporate the age of a car into their pricing decision.[77] Furthermore, it is explained how the pricing behavior varies between heterogeneous sellers. It is investigated how the size of the anchoring effect depends on individuals' experience and income level. The focus of the analyses is to find out whether professional sellers are aware of individuals' exposedness to the anchoring heuristic and can take advantage of their knowledge. The conducted investigations provide insight into the functioning and price-formation process in secondary markets and explain why the observed asking prices of used cars differ from the car values that include all relevant information and explicitly take the exact car age into account.

The findings of this study are as follows: First, by analyzing within-year price effects during the registration year, significant price differences for cars of the same age that only differ in their month of their initial registration are found.[78] At first glance, this is a surprising result because a price effect of the initial registration month seems implausible. Second, detailed empirical evidence is provided that these price differences are the result of an anchoring heuristic employed by the market participants in the secondary market to simplify their pricing decisions. An explanation for this price effect is that the price of a used car depends on the average price of comparable cars that were initially registered in the same year. Therefore, on average, prices of cars that were first-time registered early in a year are overvalued because they are older than the average car of the same vintage, whereas, on average, used cars that were first-time registered late in a year are offered for sale below their adequate values because they are newer than the average car of the same vintage. As a consequence, with an average price difference of several hundred euros, the price difference between two cars that differ only in their month of the initial

---

[77]The anchoring heuristic was first introduced by Tversky and Kahneman (1974).
[78]In Germany, the date of the first registration is officially documented at the vehicle registration certificate.

registration can be substantial even though both cars are the same age. In this case, the cars were offered for sale at different points in time. However, including time fixed effects to control for the time of the advertisements' listing date, the registration months' price effect is still existent. Third, although both commercial and private sellers are subjected to heuristic information processing, it is shown that professional car dealers are better able than private sellers to take advantage of market participants' heuristic information processing. This provides evidence for information asymmetries in the used-car market because it can be verified that car dealers are aware of individuals' limited information processing and therefore better informed than private sellers. Finally, it is detected that the relative price discrepancies between the asking price and adequate value are greater for low-priced cars indicating that the size of the anchoring effect depends on households' income level and cognitive abilities.

These investigations are highly relevant in many respects. Heuristic decision rules appear not only in the used-car market but also in all markets that are affected by inefficient information processing.[79] Individuals' limited cognitive abilities often make it impossible to incorporate all relevant information into a decision process or the information evaluation is too costly. It is therefore all the more important to assess the consequences of the applied decision rule. For example, using the setting of the used-car market, important insights for leasing institutions and banks are provided. The risk management of these financial institutions should consider the obtained results in their risk assessment because market prices can significantly vary from their expected model-based predictions. Furthermore, guidance for prospective sellers and buyers of both new and used cars is offered. Therefore, the results of this study are both highly important and of general interest.

This chapter proceeds as follows. In the next section, an overview about the literature of heuristic information processing and price anomalies with focus on the automobile market is given. In Section 4.3, the hypotheses are derived, which are the focus of the

---

[79]For example, Chetty et al. (2009) and Finkelstein (2009) find evidence for limited information processing by analyzing taxes and tolls, Kandel et al. (2001), DellaVigna and Pollet (2009) and Hirshleifer et al. (2009) confirm these findings for financial markets and Malmendier and Lee (2011) and Brown et al. (2010) verify these results for Internet auctions.

investigation. Section 4.4 gives an overview of the data set, which is used for the empirical analyses in Section 4.5. Finally, concluding remarks are offered in Section 4.6.

4.2 Literature Review

In the literature, some studies document the role of information provision. Tadelis and Zettelmeyer (2015) measure the effect of information disclosure on automobile auctions outcomes and find higher revenues as soon as more information is provided. Similar results are obtained by Kagel and Levin (1986) and Levin et al. (1996), who use laboratory experiments to show that information disclosure results in higher revenues. Lewis (2011) notes that information provision reduces adverse selection and information asymmetries in online markets.

A related stream in the literature shows that individuals' information processing is limited. Although all relevant information about a product is observable, individuals do not behave rationally. For example, Malmendier and Lee (2011) provide evidence of limited attention in online auctions because the outcome of an auction sometimes exceeds observable fixed prices that are available on the same website. Bidders' irrational behavior is explained by an irrelevant outside retail price in the description of the product details that is used for the evaluation of the products. Evidence of limited attention in financial markets can be found in Gilbert et al. (2012) (who show that investors focus on summary statistics instead of the evaluation of individual information) and DellaVigna and Pollet (2009). The latter ascertain an under-reaction in the stock markets to information announced on Fridays.

Price anomalies in the used-car market are analyzed by Kooreman and Haan (2006), Lacetera et al. (2012) and Englmaier et al. (2017). The observation that used cars' prices depend rather on calendar years than on months has first been made by Kooreman and Haan (2006). However, their data set was much less impressive and their empirical strategy is not convincing (e.g. the age is modeled by a linear term). Lacetera et al. (2012) find evidence of a left-digit bias in the processing of odometer value, leading to systematic and substantial price drops at 10,000-mile odometer thresholds. They analyze more than 22 million wholesale used-car transactions and detect that individuals focus on the leftmost digits when assessing car value.[80] The analysis of Englmaier et al. (2017) documents systematic and substantial price drops at vintage thresholds.

Related to the topic of the present study is the experimental analysis of Bergman et al. (2010). They show that an increase in individuals' cognitive ability decreases the size of the anchoring effect. The present study of this chapter is able to verify their results in a real market setting. Additionally, it is shown that sellers' experience and information level can even increase the size of the anchoring effect if this increases sellers' profits. In this case, well-informed sellers deliberately exploit that less-experienced individuals are exposed to anchoring.

The study of this chapter contributes to the literature of heuristic evaluation rules. Empirical evidence for the existence of heuristic thinking and limited information processing in a real market setting is found and the price effects on used cars is directly measured. Studies primarily provide experimental evidence of the existence of heuristics and focus on surveys and laboratory experiments. Only few studies analyze the price effects and market implication of these simplifying decision rules.[81] Moreover, the results of this chapter indicate that the used-car market is characterized by information asymmetries. Akerlof (1970) demonstrates the implications for used-car markets in which sellers are better informed than buyers about the quality of used cars: Either bad products will drive out good products or the sellers of used cars will invest in signaling their quality to buyers (see also Akerlof (1976), Bond (1982) and Lewis (2011)). The results of this chapter show how products pricing is affected by well-informed car dealers and less-informed households. This is the first study that analyzed whether individuals' exposing to heuristic decision rules is deliberately exploited by professional market participants in a real market. The results give insights into the price-formation process with heterogeneous agents.

---

[80]See Poltrock and Schwartz (1984) and Korvorst and Damian (2008) about the evaluation of multi-digit numbers and Basu (1997) and Basu (2006) about the literature on 99-cent pricing.

[81]See Lacetera et al. (2012), Englmaier and Schmöller (2010) and Pope (2009).

4.3 Hypotheses

In this section, several hypotheses about the effects of individuals' limited information processing on their evaluation of used cars are derived, which leads to discrepancies between the observed asking prices and the used-car values that contain all relevant information. The hypotheses will be tested in Section 4.5 using used-car advertisements on the Internet platform AutoScout24. Internet platforms are one of the most important sales channels in the automobile industry. By using the search mask with default options on the AutoScout24 website, prospective car buyers and sellers can screen all available advertisements for car specific criteria, such as brand, model and registration year. An advanced search function enables filtering for mileage, fuel-type, gear transmission, power and other more specific criteria. A direct screening of car age is impossible because the search function only allows filtering for the year of the first registration (2016, 2015,...) although the year and month of the initial registration are reported on the website.[82] Hence, filtering for car age can only be done approximately by the year of the first-time registration and the total age of each used car has to be individually calculated by prospective car buyers and sellers and is not directly observable. In some car markets a new model is issued every year and the model year can be used as an approximation for the registration year. However, in Europe, new car models are introduced at different points in time and not once a year. For this reason, the month of the models' introduction date differs from model to model. Filtering for the model year is not possible on the AutoScout24 website.

To evaluate a car, sellers can compare Internet platforms' prices for used cars that are similar to their own vehicle to determine a reference value.[83] However, the search results for a car model of a certain vintage often provide hundreds or thousands of matches. If

---

[82]This is not a specific characteristic of AutoScout24 website; instead, it is a general attribute for the search function in online used-car markets (see e.g., http://www.cars.com or http://www.nadaguides.com; last accessed: January 27, 2016).

[83]Alternatives to Internet platforms' prices for the evaluation of used cars are directories of second-hand car valuations, e.g., as in the case of the German used-car market, the 'Schwacke Liste' or the 'Deutsche Automobil Treuhand' (DAT). However, the car valuation of Schwacke is not freely available and DAT does only provide the dealer purchase value and, furthermore, does not take into account all relevant factors influencing the used-car price. Hence, Internet used-car platforms will be used as the primary source of information.

a prospective car seller wants to correctly evaluate a car of a given registration month of a given registration year, he has to browse through all matches of similar cars of the same vintage and compare only the advertisements of the same registration month, which is very time-consuming because of a missing search filter for the month of the initial registration or the car age, which is generally not provided by Internet used-car platforms. Therefore, the evaluation of a used car is expected not to be based on the actual car age, but instead on all reported search results of similar cars in the same registration year. However, it is supposed that this effect is not merely caused by the restrictions of the search mask; instead, they arise from individuals' own simplifying assumptions related to car age. Therefore, individuals might use the year of the initial registration as an approximation of car age. For these reasons, the estimated price of a used car might be similar to the average price of comparable cars with the same initial registration year as a consequence of the search results and individuals' simplifying assumptions. Thus, sellers might tend to anchor the average price of cars with the same initial registration year, which in turn might be used as a reference value in their valuation process. [84]

Consequently, a within-year price analysis of the year of the initial registration might provide evidence whether individuals are exposed to the anchoring heuristic, which results in over- and undervaluation of used cars. To measure the price discrepancy between the car value that contains all relevant information (adequate_car_value) and individuals' price estimation (asking_price) for car i, the variable $pgap_i$ is introduced, which is defined as follows:

$$pgap_i := asking\_price_i - adequate\_car\_value_i, \tag{4.1}$$

where $asking\_price_i$ is the advertised price for car i at the website of the Internet platform and $adequate\_car\_value_i$ is defined as the value of car i, which considers all relevant and available information about the car (especially actual age). It can be expected that the asking prices of cars initially registered in the first half of a year exceed adequate

---

[84] It cannot be expected that prospective car sellers exactly calculate the mean value of all listed advertisements of their search results. However, car sellers get a feeling about the average car value by screening the search results. Against this background, this assessment will be used as the reference value in the following.

value because individuals' price-formation process is affected by newer cars. For example, consider a car that was first-time registered in January. In that situation, all similar cars of the same vintage are newer or of the same age than this car, resulting in an expected sales price that is higher than adequate value. For these reasons, the following price discrepancy hypothesis is considered:

> *Price discrepancy hypothesis (H1a): On average, advertisements for used cars that were initially registered in the first half of a year are overvalued (pgap > 0).*

Analogously, it can be expected that cars whose first-time registration occurred in the second half of a year are undervalued.[85] Therefore, the following price discrepancy hypothesis is suggested:

> *Price discrepancy hypothesis (H1b): On average, advertisements for used cars that were initially registered in the second half of a year are undervalued (pgap < 0).*

The absolute discrepancy between adequate value and estimated used-car value (asking price) should be the greatest if the car was first-time registered in January or December because the average price of cars of the same vintage might be equal to the prices of cars that were registered in June and July. It can therefore be expected that the price discrepancy (*pgap*) decreases during a registration year (January to December). This means that the absolute value of the price discrepancy (|*pgap*|) increases the further the initial registration date is from the middle of the year. This elicits the anchoring heuristic. Therefore, the following anchoring hypothesis is suggested:

> *Anchoring hypothesis (H1c): On average, the price discrepancy (pgap) decreases the later in the year that the car was initially registered.*

Next, it is focused on the considerations about heterogeneity in sellers with respect to their information and experience. Two different seller types can be observed. On the one hand, cars are advertised by professional car dealers; on the other hand, cars are also advertised by probably less-informed households. It can be expected that car dealers are better informed not only because of their enhanced abilities to observe the used-car

---

[85]For example, a car initially registered in December 2010 is newer than a car that was initially registered in June 2010.

market and closer customer contacts but also because they benefit from their years of experience. This may indicate that the observable discrepancies in dealers' car advertisements are either not measurable or only small because of those sellers' superior abilities to correctly evaluate a car. However, in the study, it is assumed that car dealers are aware of this anchoring effect and the limited information processing of some market participants and exploit individuals' inattention to the correct car age for their own benefit.

For this reason, it can be expected that professional car dealers deliberately set higher-than-adequate-value prices for used cars that were initially registered between January and June. If evidence for hypotheses H1a, H1b and H1c can be found, it cannot be expected that households are aware of their limited attention to actual car age in general because otherwise the asking prices would reflect the effective car age and price discrepancies would not be observed. Thus, private sellers that correctly evaluate their used cars either will not take advantage of this heuristic decision rule (advertising their cars for adequate value) or will represent only a relatively small proportion of sellers compared to professional car dealers.

Therefore, it is expected that the average price discrepancies are higher for dealers' advertisements of used cars that were initially registered during the first half of a year. This would give evidence for information asymmetries in the used-car market because unlike private sellers, professional sellers are aware of this heuristic. The expectation about the different pricing behavior of car dealers and households is summarized in the following information asymmetry hypothesis:

Information asymmetry hypothesis (H2a): The price discrepancy (pgap) is greater for dealers' used-car advertisements than for households' used-car advertisements if the car was initially registered during the first half of a year.

In contrast, well-informed car dealers will demand adequate value for cars registered between July and December because this value is greater than the reference value of all cars of the same vintage. Professional sellers are not willing to sell their cars at less than adequate value. However, because higher prices than the reference value are only enforceable to a certain extent and a few car dealers are less-informed, smaller price discrepancies are expected in dealers' advertisements.[86] Nevertheless, it is assumed that the absolute price discrepancy ($|pgap|$) is smaller for cars advertised by dealers than for cars advertised by households. Therefore, the following information asymmetry hypothesis is suggested:

> *Information asymmetry hypothesis (H2b): The absolute price discrepancy ($|pgap|$) is smaller for dealers' used-car advertisements than for households' used-car advertisements if the car was initially registered during the second half of a year.*

Finally, the impact of individuals' cognitive abilities on the extent of individuals' limited information processing is considered. Therefore, the size of the anchoring effect for cars of different price levels is analyzed. Bergman et al. (2010) show that an increase in individuals' cognitive ability decreases the size of the anchoring effect. High-priced cars are mostly traded by well-educated people, which should decrease the anchoring effect compared to advertisements of low-priced cars. This investigation gives insights into the inattention level of households of different income level to the actual car age.

Naturally, the absolute price discrepancy increases the higher a car's price level is. For this reason, relative prices have to be compared. Hence, it is expected that the relative price discrepancy is greater for low-cost cars because of a higher inattention of low-income households. For example, a price discrepancy of €50 would not be the crucial factor in buyers' purchase decision even if the car's price is very low. Therefore, low-income households are less sensitive to relative changes from the adequate car value than high-income households because the absolute price discrepancy is very low compared to the absolute price discrepancy of high-income households. Moreover, this presumption is corroborated by Busse et al. (2013b), who find a higher inattention level to the current odometer value for low-income buyers than for high-income buyers. The following cognitive ability hypothesis concludes the made assumptions:

> *Cognitive ability hypothesis (H3): The absolute value of the relative price discrepancy ($|pgap_{rel}| := |ln(asking\_price) - ln(adequate\_car\_value)|$) is greater for price advertisements for low-cost cars than the relative price discrepancy for expensive cars.*

---

[86]It is assumed that these higher-than-reference-value prices are enforceable because dealer advertisements include guarantees and are therefore slightly different from private offerings for sale.

In the next section, the data set will be presented, which is used for the empirical analysis in Section 4.5.

4.4 Description of the Data Set

To analyze the hypotheses presented in the section above, a data set of nearly seven million used-car advertisements provided by AutoScout24, Europe's largest Internet platform of new and used cars, which serves as an intermediary between buyers and sellers, is employed. This data set consists of used-car advertisements in the German submarket. Car sellers can list their vehicles on this Internet platform without paying a fee.[87] The search function enables prospective car buyers to screen all car advertisements related to their preferred car characteristics. Using the search mask with default options, they can filter for car brand, model, year of initial registration and location of seller. A detail search also allows filtering for criteria, such as asking price and a range of mileage driven, fuel type, power, etc.[88] One important observation is the sole existence of a filter for the year of the initial registration and not for screening car age. Both buyers and sellers can use the search results to assess the market price of the car that they want to sell or buy.

Unlike Lacetera et al. (2012), who analyze heuristic information processing by using wholesale-auction prices, the final transaction prices cannot be observed but the asking prices. Consequently, because of price negotiations, the asking prices listed in this data set could vary from the real transaction prices. Nevertheless, it can be expected that this issue should not cause any problems for the interpretations of the results of the empirical study for the following reasons:[89] The focus of the study of this chapter is to analyze used-car market participants' information processing. Asking price reveals their assessment of the market value of the car that they want to sell in the secondary market. Moreover, price negotiations should influence all prices in the car advertisements in the data set to

---

[87]The number of free car advertisements is limited to two. Source: https://angebot.autoscout24.de/marktplatz; last accessed: January 27, 2016.

[88]For a complete overview see: https://www.autoscout24.com; last accessed: January 27, 2016.

[89]Other studies also incorporate asking prices in their analyses. See for example Englmaier et al. (2017).

approximately the same extent. For this reason, only systematic price effects are expected, which cannot explain price effects of the months of the initial registration date. Different price effects for used cars, which differ in the month of their initial registration, caused by price negotiations, are implausible.[90] Morton et al. (2011) identify that price negotiations are mainly influenced by comparisons of similar offers and the final customers' knowledge about the reservation price. Hence, asking prices should not present a problem for these analyses.

Furthermore, the used-car market is very competitive and therefore sellers will not set their required prices much higher than their expectations about the car's value or comparable market values because otherwise, potential used-car buyers will not be attracted. According to Hanemann (1991), Shogren et al. (1994) and Englmaier et al. (2017), in such a market setting the asking price is unlikely to differ from willingness to pay. Although some individuals certainly might not behave rationally, nearly 90% of the cars in the data set were advertised by professional car dealers. Because of their expertise, apart from the price discrepancy caused by neglecting actual car age, a correct price assessment of their advertised cars can be expected and because of the Internet used-car platforms' search functions, this is even expected to be the case for households' advertisements because they can use search results as a reference for their own pricing. According to Kahneman et al. (1991), List (2003) and List (2004) a divergence between the willingness to pay and the willingness to accept is unlikely to apply in a market environment dominated by car dealers that purchase cars for resale instead for use.

The used data set consists of 7,727,267 used-car advertisements placed between 2009-2011 on the German website of AutoScout24. The information about sales offerings were provided by AutoScout24 on a quarterly basis and include each car's asking price, odometer value, date of the first-time registration,[91] engine power, fuel type, brand and model, along with whether the car was advertised by a professional car dealer or by a private sellers. 111 different car brands and 1,472 different car models can be observed, which is

---

[90] A correlation of the negotiation range and the bias of the adequate value regarding the month of the initial registration is not expected. Otherwise, market participants would be aware of the bias, leading to a correct used-car valuation. However, substantial price discrepancies are observable.

[91] Car age is not directly observable but can be calculated from the date of first-time registration.

a very good approximation of the German used-car market because it contains almost all of the car models that are available in this market. To manage implausible observations, which might be a result of some individuals' typing errors when placing car advertisements on the AutoScout24 website, the data is truncated for each car classification by excluding 1% of the cars with the highest mileage and 1% of the cars with the highest and lowest engine power. The same is done for the asking price for each car classification using again the vehicle classification by the Commission of the European Communities (see Table 2.1).

As a result of excluding these car advertisements, it is also considered that asking prices are studied: some overpriced cars will not be demanded by prospective used-car buyers. By truncating the data set, the obtained results are not exposed to biases caused by unrealistically high prices and very low prices, which might be attributed to car damages for which it is not possible to control. Moreover, the data set is restricted to cars that are less than 15 years old. Very old cars are eliminated because of their small numbers of observations and because automobile enthusiasts selling classic cars demand very high prices for which it is not possible to control. However, because it is not the purpose of this study to analyze classic cars' prices, this issue should not present a problem. Furthermore, the data set is restricted to offers of passenger cars, deleting advertisements of both trucks (above 3.5 t) and motorbikes. Only cars with a gasoline or diesel engine are used and advertisements of cars with missing records of some variables are omitted. After applying these restrictions, the data set consists of 6,922,846 observations.

For an overview of the data set, some descriptive statistics of the relevant variables are presented. Table 4.1 lists summary statistics for the variables *age, mileage, engine power* and *asking price*.

In Table 4.2, an overview of car-specific dummy variables is given. Noticeably, nearly 90% of cars were advertised by professional car dealers. The distribution of the registration month is similar to the distribution of new car registrations in Germany: More cars were

Table 4.1: **Summary Statistics - Continuous Variables**
This table presents summary statistics for the variables *age, mileage, power* and *asking price*. The age is measured in years, mileage in thousand kilometers, power in kilowatt, the asking price in euros.

Variable	Mean	Sd	Min	p25	p50	p75	Max
Age	4.09	3.68	0.00	0.98	3.19	6.07	15.00
Mileage	63.52	57.28	0.00	15.46	48.00	99.34	316.30
Power	96.84	42.76	31.00	71.00	88.00	110.00	420.00
Asking price	16,287.27	13,175.91	425.00	7,990.00	13,490.00	20,670.00	205,900.00

registered in spring than in summer and winter.[92] Therefore, it can be expected that the data set is not biased by some under- or overrepresented months of initial registration.

Furthermore, for different sales dates, the distribution of the registration month does not change significantly. This indicates that the sales month is not correlated with the initial registration month.

4.5 Empirical Results

In this section, the hypotheses from Section 4.3 are tested, which refer to price distortions of used cars caused by limited information processing regarding actual car age, using OLS regression methods with robust standard errors. Inflation-adjusted asking prices are used as the dependent variable in the regression analyses. Because of the Akaike information criterion (AIC), the explanatory variable *age* is modeled by a 6th-order polynomial.[93] For the control variables of *mileage* and *power*, linear and quadratic terms attributable to the higher impact of price deterioration for the initial kilometers and a higher appreciation of each kilowatt for cars with less-powerful engines are used.[94] Time fixed effects are applied, which correspond to the advertisements' listing date, to control for seasonality

---

[92] Compare to Federal Motor Transport Authority: http://www.kba.de; last accessed: January 27, 2016.

[93] For some analyses, logarithmized asking prices are utilized. Based on the AIC, which is also suggested by Englmaier et al. (2017), an 8th-order age polynomial is implemented for these regressions. See also Appendix 4.7.1 for further details regarding the AIC.

[94] Non-linear depreciation rates are also suggested in the literature. See, e.g., Wykoff (1970), Ackerman (1973) and Ohta and Griliches (1976).

Table 4.2: **Summary Statistics - Categorical Variables**
This table lists car-specific dummy variables for 6,922,846 online used-car
advertisements. The vehicle classification of the Commission of the European
Communities is used.

	Obs.	Percentage
Fuel		
Petrol	4,024,810	58.14
Diesel	2,898,036	41.86
Seller		
Dealer	6,114,520	88.32
Private	808,326	11.68
Car classification		
Mini cars	325,618	4.70
Small cars	999,097	14.43
Medium cars	1,739,712	25.13
Large cars	1,469,118	21.22
Executive cars	502,721	7.26
Luxury cars	99,313	1.43
Sport utility cars	424,688	6.13
Sport coupes	259,227	3.74
Multi-purpose cars	1,103,352	15.94
Registration month		
January	506,190	7.31
February	511,818	7.39
March	725,818	10.48
April	604,309	8.73
May	627,832	9.07
June	678,654	9.80
July	545,909	7.89
August	483,369	6.98
September	585,956	8.46
October	558,890	8.07
November	566,270	8.18
December	527,831	7.62

in consumer demand and supply and economic developments. Car fixed effects control for the car model. The car's model year is not observable in this data set.

4.5.1 Anchoring in the Used-Car Market

In this section, the price effect of individuals' limited information processing in their assessment of the value of their used cars when evaluating car age is analyzed. The analysis begins with a detailed examination of the effect of the month of the initial registration on the prices of used cars and investigate whether individuals tend to anchor on the average car value of comparable cars of the same initial registration year, leading to over- and undervaluation of used cars. It would be reasonable to assume that the month of a car's initial registration date should not affect its price in the used-car market. Nonetheless, as derived in Section 4.3, it is proposed that individuals tend to anchor on the average car value of comparable cars of the same vintage, causing price discrepancies in the used-car market attributable to limited information processing regarding actual car age. Therefore, it can be assumed that, on average, cars that were initially registered in the first half of a year are overvalued and cars that were initially registered in the second half of a year are undervalued.

In the first step, a graphical analysis of price effects of the initial registration month during a car's lifecycle is performed. For this reason the age of each car is normalized in such a way that the normalized age contains the age of each car in number of months normalized to the first day of the year at which it was offered for sale. This means that all cars that were initially registered in December of the year prior to the year in which they were offered for sale are treated as one-month-old cars. Cars that were initially registered in November of the year prior to the year they were advertised in the secondary market are treated as two-month-old cars and so forth. Cars that were initially registered in the same year in which they were offered for sales are excluded in this graphical analysis. By using these adjustments, the vintage thresholds can be clearly illustrated and easily identified at each multiple of twelve months. The variable age_{norm}, which contains the normalized age, is introduced as described below:

$$age_{norm} = 12 \cdot (sales\_year - reg\_year - 1) + (13 - reg\_month) \qquad (4.2)$$

where $reg\_year \in \{2010, 2009, ...\}$ and $reg\_month \in \{1, 2, ..., 12\}$ indicate the year and month in which the car was first-time registered; $sales\_year \in \{2009, 2010, 2011\}$ specifies the year that the car was advertised on the AutoScout24 website. For reasons of clarity, cars that were offered for sale in the same year as they were registered for the first time are not considered in the graphical analysis, but later in the regression analysis. To ensure that all cars of the same normalized age are nearly the same age, for the graphical analysis, the data set is restricted to car advertisements that were offered during the same quarter regardless of whether the sales year is the same. The data set is divided by quarters and the graphical analysis is performed separately for each of the subsets.[95] Otherwise, the large difference in the actual age of cars that, for example, were offered for sale in the first and in the fourth quarter of a year could bias the results.[96]

To analyze the within-year price effect of a registration year, the average raw asking prices are calculated controlling for all of the observable car characteristics of the data set. The resulting average adjusted asking prices are the average residuals of a registration month for each normalized age, which can be interpreted as the averages of the price discontinuities ($pgap_i$) for all cars i of a registration month as defined in Equation 4.1. In other words, the forecast of the $asking\_price_i$ for car i is used, which results from a regression model in which all available car characteristics are employed as independent variables, to obtain an approximation of the $adequate\_car\_value_i$. The obtained residuals should not show any systematic pattern, but should be normally distributed around

---

[95] The graphical analysis were performed for all four quarters, but the results did not change substantially. For that reason, only the results of the car advertisements from the third quarter of a year are presented as an arbitrary example.

[96] The actual age of a car offered for sale in January and first-time registered in December of the previous year is one month equals the normalized age, but the actual age of a car which was offered for sale in December and first-time registered in December of the previous year is twelve months which is unequal to the normalized age of one month.

the horizontal axis. Figure 4.1 shows the plot of the monthly average residuals of cars of the same normalized age.

A linear trend of the average residuals is added for each registration year interval. For all of these intervals, an increasing relationship of the average residuals can be found within a single registration year. This means that the average prediction of car value, which is based on exact car age, is much higher than the real asking prices for cars that were initially registered in the second half of a year (Jul-Dec) and much lower than the asking prices of cars that were initially registered in the first half of a year (Jan-Jun). Therefore, it can be concluded that on average, used cars are underpriced if they were first-time registered late in a year and overpriced if they were first-time registered early in a year, which is in line with the price discrepancy hypotheses (H1a) and (H1b). The slope of the linear trends supports the anchoring hypothesis (H1c).

To test whether these observed monthly patterns cause statistically significant price effects in the used-car market, regression analyses are performed with dummy variables that indicate the month in which a car was registered for the first time by taking the following form:

$$price_i = \alpha + \beta'month_i + f(a_i) + \gamma'X_i + \epsilon_i, \tag{4.3}$$

where $price_i$ corresponds to the asking price of car i and the vector $month_i$ contains the dummy variables for January to December to indicate the month of the first registration. $f(a_i)$ describes a function of the car age and X_i contains all of the other relevant characteristics of car i. Table 4.3 reports the results of the regression analyses with robust standard errors by using June as the basis month. To control for the age of the car, a 6th-order age polynomial is implemented based on the Akaike information criterion, as noted above.

Regression (E.1) uses the complete data set, whereas regression (E.2) is only implemented for car advertisements of professional car dealers and regression (E.3) for households' advertisements. Obviously, on average, all of the prices of cars that were initially

Figure 4.1: **Residuals - Registration Year Discontinuities**
This figure plots the average residuals of all raw asking prices that have the
same normalized age after controlling for all available car information. The
age of each car is normalized to the first day of the year they were offered
for sale to obtain a registration year threshold at each 12-month interval
(vertical lines). Only observations that were advertised in the same quarter
are used to ensure that all used cars that were first-time registered in the
same month and year are nearly of the same age. The left-most dot of each
registration year interval contains the average residual value for cars that
were first-time registered in December.

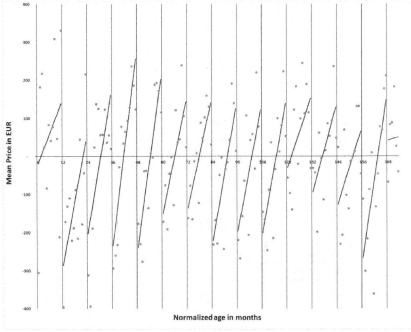

Table 4.3: **Anchoring in the Used-Car Market**
This table lists the results of OLS regressions with robust standard errors for the data set of nearly seven million used-car advertisements of an Internet platform. Dummy variables are used for each month to measure the impact of the month of the initial registration on the used-car prices. Regression (E.1) employs the complete data set, regression (E.2) restricts the data set to advertisements of professional car dealers and regression (E.3) restricts the data set to households' used-car advertisements. All of the regressions use June as the basis month. The symbols †,*,**,*** indicate statistical significance at the 10%, 5%, 1% and 0.1% level, respectively.

	(E.1)	(E.2)	(E.3)
	Full sample	Dealer	Private
Registration month			
Jan	304.234***	341.229***	87.339***
	(8.557)	(9.198)	(16.205)
Feb	177.322***	192.900***	51.380**
	(8.319)	(8.905)	(16.072)
Mar	175.958***	178.749***	100.599***
	(7.74)	(8.305)	(14.96)
Apr	205.885***	215.296***	91.961***
	(7.972)	(8.607)	(15.505)
May	52.919***	40.882***	94.524***
	(7.848)	(8.457)	(15.267)
Jul	-25.130**	-12.711	-91.210***
	(8.412)	(9.119)	(15.612)
Aug	-49.620***	-48.344***	-76.104***
	(8.322)	(8.957)	(15.987)
Sep	-75.892***	-69.862***	-150.517***
	(7.993)	(8.546)	(15.827)
Oct	-69.816***	-55.424***	-211.919***
	(8.136)	(8.751)	(15.549)
Nov	-82.877***	-65.081***	-221.930***
	(8.042)	(8.612)	(15.494)
Dec	-295.378***	-298.876***	-269.824***
	(8.101)	(8.701)	(15.42)
6th-order age polynomial	Yes	Yes	Yes
Controls for car characteristics	Yes	Yes	Yes
Car-fixed effects	Yes	Yes	Yes
Time-fixed effects	Yes	Yes	Yes
Constant	21661.188***	21553.847***	20854.052***
	(220.631)	(308.089)	(260.807)
Observations	6,922,846	6,114,520	808,326
R^2	0.883	0.884	0.884
Adjusted R^2	0.883	0.884	0.884

registered in the months January to May are significantly higher than the car prices of the basis month June (€52.92 to €304.23) and significantly lower (€–25.13 to €–295.38) for cars that were initially registered in other months (July to December). Moreover, the absolute price discrepancy increases the higher the absolute difference in months from the basis month. For this reason, potential used-car buyers should prefer to buy cars that were registered late in a year. Average savings can be several hundred euros. For example, the price difference between two similar cars of the same age that were first-time registered in January and December is €600 on average. In contrast, potential buyers of new cars should register their car for the first time early in a year to increase their car's resale value. These findings support the price discrepancy hypotheses (H1a), (H1b) and the anchoring hypothesis (H1c) and give empirical and statistical evidence for within-year price effects caused by the month of the initial registration. Hence, the systematic patterns of Figure 4.1 are a result of the heuristic thinking of individuals who tend to anchor their assessment of the car value on the average value of similar cars of the same vintage. Additionally, to show that these findings do not contradict the results of Englmaier et al. (2017), who find price discontinuities regarding the vehicle age at vintage threshold, in Appendix 4.7.2, the results of Englmaier et al. (2017) are replicated as a robustness check.

4.5.2 Exploiting Anchoring by Professional Sellers

In this section, it is analyzed whether the size of the anchoring effect differs between professional car dealers and private sellers. The main object of this investigation is to examine whether some market participants are aware of the existence of individuals' usage of the anchoring heuristic and the price effects of the month of the initial registration as presented in Section 4.5.1 and can take advantage of their knowledge. This would give evidence for information asymmetries in the used-car market. As derived in Section 4.3, it is assumed that professional car dealers are better informed than private sellers because of their superior experience and their better customer contacts. For this reason, it is expected that the absolute discrepancies of dealers' price demands for cars that were initially registered in the second half of a year are lower than the absolute discrepancies of households' price demands for such cars. This would increase car dealers' profits because they sell these cars above the average price of similar cars of the same vintage. For cars that were initially registered in the first half of a year, the opposite is expected: Car dealers that are aware of the price effect of the month of the initial registration date will not demand the adequate value of these cars because potential buyers of these cars base their car valuation on the average price of similar cars of the same vintage and consequently are prepared to pay more-than-adequate-value prices for cars that were first-time registered at the beginning of the year. For this reason, car dealers deliberately offer such cars for sale at higher prices than their adequate values. Therefore, overvaluation is expected to be much higher for dealers' car advertisements than for cars that were offered for sale by private sellers. To verify these conjectures, first, a graphical analysis of the coefficients of the dummy variables for each month of the initial registration is presented, as listed in Table 4.3. Figure 4.2 plots the average price discrepancies for each month, distinguishing between dealers' and households' car advertisements.

As expected, absolute price discrepancies are much higher for car dealers than for households if the car was initially registered in the first half of a year and lower if the car was initially registered in the second half of a year. Only the coefficients of May and December are not in line with the made assumptions. Whereas the difference of the price discrepancies between dealers' and households' advertisements for these two months are relatively small, the coefficient of the dummy variable for cars which were first-time registered in December and advertised by car dealers is very low compared to the other months. This result is surprising and requires further investigation. One possible explanation of this effect is that in December, car dealers register comparatively more new cars only for a very short period (for example, for a single day) than in the other months. The purpose of these short-term registrations is to give customers higher discounts because the car becomes a used car even though it has not been driven in road traffic. It is therefore an instrument to increase the sales of both car dealers and automobile manufacturers. Because car dealers must fulfill given sales figures, which are likely linked to bonus payments by automobile manufacturers, they can use this instrument to increase their

Figure 4.2: **Price Discrepancy: The Impact of the Month of the Initial Registration**

This figure plots the coefficients of the dummy variables for the month of the initial regression from Table 4.3, distinguishing between car advertisements of professional car dealers (regression (E.2)) and those of households (regression (E.3)). The basis month of the regressions is June.

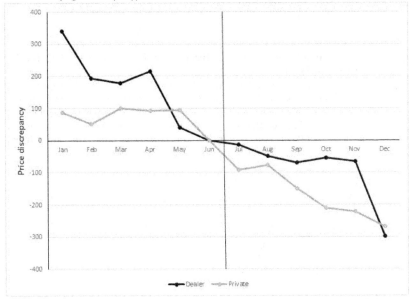

sales. This implies that in the group of cars that were first-time registered in December, the share of cars that had a short-term registration is considerably higher than the share of cars that were first-time registered in other months. This leads to lower average prices for these cars because of higher discounts, which is a possible explanation for the extreme price discrepancy for cars that were first-time registered in December and advertised by car dealers, as observed in Figure 4.2.[97]

---

[97]The Federal Motor Transport Authority reports a higher proportion of new-car registrations in automotive trade and repair in December compared to the annual average: http://www.kba.de/DE/Statistik/Fahrzeuge/Neuzulassungen/MonatlicheNeuzulassungen/ monatl_neuzulassungen_node.html; last accessed: January 27, 2016. In the AutoScout24 data set, it can also be found that the proportion of dealers' advertisements of cars newer than one year is the highest for cars that were first registered in December.

To verify the presumptions about the average price of cars that were initially registered in December, the average price discrepancies is measured for each month using only cars that are not newer than one year and not first-time registered in December. By doing so, it can be ensured that the main influence of short-term registered cars vanishes.[98] Figure 4.3 plots the average price discrepancies for the described robustness check.

Figure 4.3: **Robustness Check - Price Discrepancy: The Impact of the Month of the Initial Registration**
This figure plots the coefficients of the dummy variables for the month of the initial regression, distinguishing between car advertisements of professional car dealers (regression (E.2)) and those of households (regression (E.3)) and using cars that are not newer than one year and that were not initially registered in December. The basis month of the regressions is June.

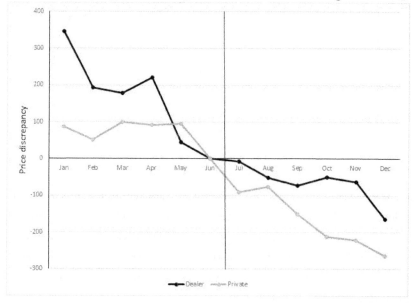

---

[98] Of course, it is possible that the prices of cars that were initially purchased as a short-term registered car and that are older than one year are below the average car value of cars that were not initially short-term registered. However, it is assumed that this effect is only very small if it exists at all.

As assumed, the absolute price discrepancy for cars that were initially registered in December declines and is more in line with the price discrepancies of the preceding months, which supports the argument above. The absolute price discrepancy is still higher for cars that were advertised by dealers and initially registered in the first half of a year than for cars that were advertised by households and lower for cars that were registered in the second half of a year. Except for the coefficients of the month August, the differences between the coefficients of dealers' and households' advertisements are significantly different from zero for all other months (p<0.001). Because August lies in the middle of a year, substantial price discrepancies between the coefficients of dealers' and households' advertisements are not expected for this month, which might explain the missing significance.

In summary, evidence for the price discrepancy hypotheses (H1a), (H1b) and the anchoring hypothesis (H1c) can be found because of higher asking prices than adequate value (which takes the exact age of a car into account) for cars that were initially registered in the first half of a year and lower asking prices than adequate value for cars that were initially registered in the second half of a year. These findings are valid for advertisements by both professional car dealers and households. The graphical analysis also confirms the information asymmetry hypotheses (H2a) and (H2b) because of the different pricing behavior between professional sellers, which can take advantage of the anchoring effects, and private sellers, which are not aware of this heuristic.

In the next step, regression analyses are used to estimate the different slope coefficients that describe the curves in Figure 4.2 for car dealers and households. Therefore, a linear relationship between the price discrepancy and the month of first-time registration is assumed and different slope parameters for the first and the second halves of a year are considered. For this reason, a dummy variable *Jan-Jun* is introduced that equals one if the car was initially registered in the first half of a year and zero if the car was initially registered in the second half of a year. To model the linear relationship between the price discrepancy and the registration month, the registration month is implemented as a discrete variable (*Month of Registration*) that equals one if the car was registered in

January, two if the car was registered in February and so on. By using interaction terms, the different pricing behavior of households and dealers in the first and second halves of a year is considered. The variable *Private* equals one if the car was advertised by a household and zero if the car was advertised by a car dealer. Advertisements of car dealers that contain cars that were first-time registered in December are excluded because of the high share of short-time registrations in this month, as described above. Table 4.4 lists the results of the performed regression analyses.

Table 4.4: **Exploiting Anchoring by Professional Sellers**
This table lists the results of OLS regressions with robust standard errors for the data set of nearly seven million used-car advertisements on an Internet platform. The month of the first-time registration is modeled as a discrete variable (*Month of Registration*), which equals one if the car was initially registered in January, two if the car was initially registered in February, etc. The variable *Private* indicates if the car was offered for sale by a household (equal one) or a professional car dealer (equal zero). The variable *Jan-Jun* is equal one if the initial registration date of a car is in the first half of a year and zero otherwise. Regression (F.1) measures the impact of the month of the initial registration for the complete data set. Regressions (F.2) and (F.3) show the results only for dealers' or households' car advertisements. Regression (F.4) uses interaction terms with the variable *Private* to measure the different pricing behavior of car dealers and households by using the complete data set. The symbols †,*,**,*** indicate statistical significance at the 10%, 5%, 1% and 0.1% level, respectively.

	(F.1)	(F.2)	(F.3)	(F.4)
	Full sample	Dealer	Private	Full sample Interaction Private
Jan-Jun × Month of Registration	-15.148***	-49.064***	28.477***	-49.046***
	(1.840)	(2.591)	(3.887)	(2.596)
Month of Registration	-38.884***	-12.043***	-39.189***	-11.143***
	(2.328)	(2.090)	(2.758)	(2.092)
Private × Month of Registration				-17.860***
				(2.596)
Jan-Jun × Month of Registration × Private				69.757***
				(5.936)
6th-order age polynomial	Yes	Yes	Yes	Yes
Controls for car characteristics	Yes	Yes	Yes	Yes
Car-fixed effects	Yes	Yes	Yes	Yes
Time-fixed effects	Yes	Yes	Yes	Yes
Constant	21794.690***	21595.383***	21065.330***	21679.721***
	(221.084)	(327.328)	(262.383)	(233.884)
Observations	6,455,618	5,647,292	808,326	6,455,618
R^2	0.884	0.885	0.884	0.884
Adjusted R^2	0.884	0.885	0.884	0.884

Regression (F.1) was performed using the complete data set, regression (F.2) uses only dealers' car advertisements, regression (F.3) only considers car advertisements by private sellers and regression (F.4) employs the whole sample by using interaction terms with the dummy variable *Private* to measure the price differences between dealers' and households' advertisements. For the sample of dealers' advertisements, a decreasing price effect of approximately €12.04 can be detected for each additional month if the car was registered in the second half (regression (F.2)). This effect increases by €49.06 if the car was registered in the first half of a year. For households' advertisements, a different pattern can be observed (regression (F.3)). The price decline for each additional month is approximately €39.19 if the car was initially registered in the second half of a year and only €10.71 (=€-39.19+€28.48) if the car was initially registered in the first half of a year. All of the coefficients are highly significant and the Wald test indicates that the effect is also significant for the first half of a year. This implies that dealers' car advertisements show higher price declines for each additional month for cars that were registered during the first half of a year (€49.06+€12.04=€61.10) than do households' car advertisements (€10.71). The opposite is true for cars that were initially registered in the second half of a year. The price decline for each additional month is much higher for households' advertisements (€39.19) than for dealers' advertisements (€12.04). This supports the information asymmetry hypotheses (H2a) and (H2b).

To verify the obtained results, also the whole data set is employed and interaction terms with the dummy variable *Private* are introduced to consider the different pricing behaviors of car dealers and households (regression (F.4)). Similar results as in regression (F.2) and regression (F.3) can be found. The price decline of each additional month for a car that was initially registered in the first half of a year is €49.05+€11.14=€60.19 for dealers' advertisements and €49.05+€11.14+€17.86-€69.76=€8.29 for households' advertisements. Both effects are highly significant according to the Wald test and confirm hypothesis (H2a). For cars that were initially registered in the second half of a year, a price decline for each additional month of €11.14 is found if the car was offered by a car dealer and a price decline of €11.14+€17.86=€29.00 if the car was offered by a household. This is in line with Figure 4.2 and supports hypothesis (H2b).

4.5.3 The Impact of Cognitive Abilities on the Size of the Anchoring Effect

Finally, price discontinuities with regard to the cars' price level are investigated to analyze the effect of sellers' cognitive abilities on the size of the anchoring effect. The purchase decision of low-income households, which are potential buyers of low-priced cars, might not depend on small absolute price differences between the asking price and adequate value such as €50. However, for low-priced cars such small absolute price differences can be high in relative terms and thus, it can be expected that relative price discontinuities are greater for low-priced cars. For this reason, a dummy variable *Low-cost* is introduced, which equals one if the car's asking price is lower than €10,000 and zero otherwise.[99] Similar to Section 4.5.2, interaction terms are implemented in the regression analyses to investigate the effect of the registration month for low-priced cars and high-priced cars in the first and second halves of a year. The regression results are reported in Table 4.5.

In regression (G.1), the asking price is employed as the dependent variable to measure absolute price effects, whereas regressions (G.2) and (G.3) use the logarithmized asking price as dependent variable to measure relative price effects. A regression analysis with logarithmized prices is implemented because the car value of low-priced cars is substantially lower than that of expensive cars. Hence, smaller absolute price discontinuities for low-priced cars could be the result of a simple size effect due to a different price level between low-priced cars and expensive cars. Regression (G.3) only considers private sellers' car advertisements and exclude dealers' advertisements. Dealers' advertisements are not included in this regression because professional sellers offer cars for sale from all car classifications and different price levels. Conclusions about their cognitive abilities are therefore not possible because they do not depend on the price level of their advertised cars. Private sellers usually advertise only one car at the same time. This enables to draw conclusions about their income level and cognitive abilities.

---

[99] Also different definitions for the dummy variable *Low-cost* were used by changing the price threshold to, for example, €12,500 or €7,500 but the results do not change substantially.

Table 4.5: **The Influence of Cognitive Ability on Anchoring**
This table lists the results of OLS regressions with robust standard errors for the data set of nearly seven million used-car advertisements on an Internet platform. The month of the first-time registration is modeled as a discrete variable (*Month of registration*), which equals one if the car was initially registered in January, two if the initial registration was in February, etc. The variable *Low-cost* indicates whether the price is below €10,000. The variable *Jan-Jun* equals one if the date of the initial registration of a car is in the first half of a year and zero otherwise. Regression (G.1) measures the different impact of the month of the initial registration on the used-car prices of low-priced and expensive cars in the first and second half of a year. Regressions (G.2) and (G.3) repeat this analysis considering logarithmized prices as dependent variable. Additionally, regression (G.3) uses only private sellers' car advertisements The symbols †,*,**,*** indicate statistical significance at the 10%, 5%, 1% and 0.1% level, respectively.

	(G.1)	(G.2)	(G.3)
	Full sample Price	Full sample Log(Price)	Private Log(Price)
Month of Registration	-50.802***	-0.0020***	-0.0027***
	(0.915)	(0.000)	(0.000)
Jan-Jun × Month of Registration	-12.067***	-0.0004***	-0.0010***
	(1.294)	(0.000)	(0.000)
Low-cost × Month of Registration	26.015***	-0.0014***	-0.0020***
	(1.205)	(0.000)	(0.000)
Jan-Jun × Low-cost × Month of Registration	13.942***	0.0008***	-0.0002
	(1.711)	(0.000)	(0.000)
6th-order age polynomial	Yes		
8th-order age polynomial		Yes	Yes
Controls for car characteristics	Yes	Yes	Yes
Car-fixed effects	Yes	Yes	Yes
Time-fixed effects	Yes	Yes	Yes
Constant	21890.792***	9.2417***	8.9234***
	(229.744)	(0.046)	(0.072)
Observations	6,455,618	6,455,618	808,326
R^2	0.884	0.942	0.913
Adjusted R^2	0.884	0.942	0.913

In regression (G.1), a highly significant positive price effect of €26.02 can be observed for each additional month if the car belongs to the group of low-priced cars because of the coefficient of the interaction term *Low cost × Month of Registration*. This means that the price discrepancy for each additional month is €26.02 smaller for low-priced cars than for other car segments. If the car was initially registered in the first half of a year, this effect increases to €39.96 (=€26.02+€13.94). Because the coefficient of the variable *Month of Registration* is –50.80 and highly significant, the price discrepancy (€–50.80+€26.02=€–24.78) continues to exist for low-priced cars that were initially registered in the second half of a year and is highly significant, according to the Wald test. The same applies to cars that were initially registered in the first half of a year (€–50.8–€12.07+€26.02+€13.94=€–22.91). As a result, it is found that the absolute price discrepancy is much higher for expensive cars, which is most likely caused by their higher prices.

The second regression (G.2), in which relative price effects are analyzed, shows different results. The coefficient of the interaction term *Low-cost × Month of Registration* is negative and highly significant, which leads to an increase in the price discrepancy for low-priced cars that were initially registered in the second half of a year by 0.14 percentage points for each additional month. The coefficient of the interaction term *Jan-Jun × Small × Month of Registration* is 0.0008 and highly significant. This means that the price discrepancy increases by 0.06 percentage points (=0.14–0.08, highly significant according to the Wald test) for each additional month for low-priced cars that were offered for sale during the first half of a year.[100]

Analyzing private sellers' advertisements in regression (G.3) shows that the price discrepancy for low-priced cars increases by 0.2 percentage points for both cars that were initially registered in the first and second halves of a year. The coefficient of the interaction term *Low-cost × Month of Registration* is negative and highly significant. As expected, this coefficient is smaller for private sellers' advertisements. This indicates a higher size of the anchoring effect for low-income households because these households mostly trade

---

[100]Lowering the threshold for *Low-cost* (<€7,500, <€5,000, <€2,500) leads to a greater relative price discrepancy for low-priced cars.

low-cost cars. In summary, the obtained findings in Table 4.5 confirm the cognitive ability hypothesis (H3) and it can be concluded that the anchoring effect decreases but does not vanish with higher cognitive ability.

4.6 Interim Results

Heuristic thinking and limited information processing are the primary reasons for price anomalies that lead to deviations in the observed market prices from the correct rational values of goods that incorporate all relevant product information. The used-car market is a prominent example of a market that contains observable price discrepancies. As illustrated by Akerlof (1970), these deviations can be caused by information asymmetries; moreover, limited information processing is considered in the literature (Lacetera et al., 2012; Englmaier et al., 2017). The study of this chapter employs a data set of approximately seven million used-car sales advertisements provided by AutoScout24, which is the largest Internet platform of used cars in Europe, to perform regression analyses. By analyzing within-year price effects, empirical evidence that individuals tend to anchor on the average car value of a vintage can be provided.

This indicates that market participants do not act on a purely rational basis. Considering the month of the initial registration, it was shown that on average, controlling for other price-relevant factors, cars that were initially registered early in a year are advertised at substantially higher prices than their adequate values and cars that were initially registered late in a year are offered for sale at lower prices than their adequate values. It can be concluded that individuals' used-car valuation is determined by the average value of similar cars of the same vintage. This gives evidence for heuristic information processing in the used-car market. Individuals are subjected to a heuristic decision rule known as anchoring.

Furthermore, it was found that professional car sellers are aware of this heuristic price formation and take advantage of individuals' limited information processing. Compared to car advertisements of private sellers, it is shown that the prices of cars that were advertised by car dealers vary much more widely from the correct car values if the car was initially registered in the first half of a year and much less if the car was initially registered in the second half of a year. This means that car dealers that are aware of individuals' limited information processing do not offer their cars for sale at the correct value, except for cars whose correct value is higher than the average value of similar cars of the same vintage. This gives evidence that professional sellers exploit anchoring to increase their profits.

Finally, it was analyzed whether the size of the anchoring effect decreases with higher cognitive abilities. The findings confirm this hypothesis because price discontinuities are substantially greater for low-priced cars, and it can be concluded that low-income households that comprise most of the potential buyers of low-priced cars pay less attention to the evaluation of the correct car age. This gives evidence that the size of the anchoring effect depends on individuals' cognitive abilities because low-priced cars are mostly traded by poorly-educated people.

The result of the presented study should be explicitly taken into account during purchase decisions by potential new and used-car buyers. Ceteris paribus, the later a car was first-time registered in a year, the greater its deterioration. Therefore, it is suggested to time the purchase of a new car in such a way that it can be registered for the first time in January because the resale values of these cars are substantially higher in the secondary market than comparable cars that were initially registered in another month. To a prospective used-car buyer, it is recommended to purchase a used car that was initially registered in December. At the extreme, the average price disparity can increase to €600.

4.7 Appendix

4.7.1 Akaike Information Criterion

The Akaike Information Criterion (AIC) is a measure to determine the relative quality of a statistical model regarding a given data set $x = (x_1, x_2, ..., x_n)$. It can be used as a model selection criterion for analyzing the data of interest. For different models, the AIC provides estimates about the quality of each model relative to each of the other models. Hence, the AIC does not reveal the general model quality in an absolute or a statistical sense. The AIC is defined by the following expression:[101]

$$AIC = -2log(\hat{\mathcal{L}}) + 2k, \tag{4.4}$$

where $\hat{\mathcal{L}}$ is the maximum value of the likelihood function of model M and k is the number of free parameters or the number of parameters that have to be estimated. The maximized value of the likelihood function of model M is determined by

$$\hat{\mathcal{L}} = max_\theta\{f(x|\theta, M)\}, \tag{4.5}$$

where $f(\cdot)$ is the joint density function of the random variables $X_1, X_2, ..., X_n$ with realizations $x = (x_1, x_2, ..., x_n)$ and θ is the unknown parameter. Regarding the AIC, the model with the minimum value is preferable.

4.7.2 Price Discontinuities: Robustness Checks

Similar to the data set of this study, Englmaier et al. (2017) also use a data set of used-car advertisements from a German online used-car market platform called mobile.de. Their data set, which is limited to the best-selling models of four German car manufacturers, consists of approximately 51,000 car advertisements. Moreover, they only consider cars older than 20 months. Hence, an analysis of the entire used-car market is still missing.

---

[101] See Akaike (1974) and Konishi and Kitagawa (2008, p. 60 ff.).

The present study observe about seven million car advertisements of all car brands and models, which were offered for sale at AutoScout24, and are able to analyze cars newer than 20 months. This is a very good approximation of the entire German used-car market. For this reason, the presented data set should be able to provide general results and extend the validity of the results of Englmaier et al. (2017) to the entire used-car market.

Price discontinuities of used cars around vintage thresholds are implausible because it means that an increase in the vehicle age by one day leads to a substantial price decline. Hence, it can be concluded that the used-car valuation is affected by market participants that do not act on a purely rational basis.

Analogously to Englmaier et al. (2017), a graphical analysis of the price effects at the registration-year thresholds during the lifecycle of a car is presented. For this reason, again, the age of each car is normalized as described in Equation 4.2. After that, the average asking prices of all cars which have the same normalized age is calculated. Figure 4.4 shows the average asking prices for each age_{norm} specifications.

Obviously, the price of a car decreases with increasing normalized age. Linear price trends are included for each vintage to illustrate the price decline within each registration year. However, after 144 month, also increasing average prices are detected, which is a reason of neglected control variables.[102] At each vintage threshold, which are indicated by the vertical lines, substantial price discontinuities can be detected. This result supports the validity of the findings of Englmaier et al. (2017) for the entire used-car market.

In a next step, regression analyses are performed to find statistical evidence for the substantial price discontinuities at vintage thresholds as shown in Figure 4.4. Referring to Lee and Lemieux (2010), a linear regression model with dummy variables is implemented to cover the price discontinuities at vintage thresholds, which has the following form:

$$price_i = \alpha + \sum_{j=0}^{n} \beta_j d_{ij} + f(a_i) + \gamma' X_i + \epsilon_i, \qquad (4.6)$$

---

[102] This graphical analysis was also performed by controlling for the car model. As a result, the linear price trends of the average car prices always decrease with increasing normalized age.

Figure 4.4: **Price Discontinuities at Vintage Thresholds**
This figure plots the average asking prices of all used-car advertisements
which have the same normalized age. The age of each car, which is expressed in months, is normalized to the first day of the year at which they
were offered for sale in order to obtain vintage thresholds at each 12-month
interval (vertical lines). Only observations that were offered for sale in the
same quarter are used to ensure that all used cars which were first-time registered in the same month and year are nearly of the same age. The left-
most dot of each registration year interval contains the average asking price
for cars which were first-time registered in December.

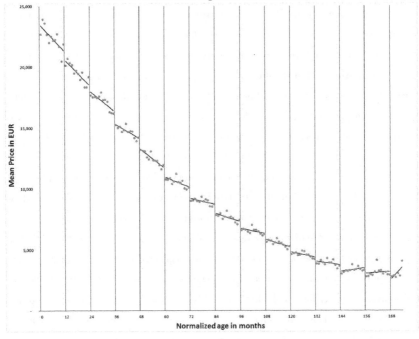

where $price_i$ corresponds to the asking price of car i and the dummy variable d_{ij} indicates if car i was first registered prior to the vintage threshold j. For example, d_{i0} indicates if car i was first registered prior to the year it was offered for sale, d_{i1} indicates if car i was registered prior to the preceding year it was offered for sale, etc. $f(a_i)$ describes a function of the car age and X_i contains all the other relevant characteristics of car i. Table 4.6 reports the results of the regression analyses with robust standard errors. To control for the age of the car, a 6th order age polynomial is implemented based on the Akaike information criterion as already mentioned.[103]

In regression (A.1), the price effect at vintage thresholds is measured when only controlling for the age of the car. Except for the dummy variable that indicates if a car was initially registered earlier than the advertisement year all dummy variables have the expected negative sign. In regressions (A.2) - (A.4), more control variables are added successively such as mileage, power and fuel-type in model (A.2), customer-type and car model in regression (A.3) and a dummy for the quarter and year when the car was advertised at the website of AutoScout24 in model (A.4). After adding all control variables into the regression equation, highly significant prices drops can be observed at every vintage threshold. Using the results of regression (A.4), it can be found that all cars that were registered earlier than the year at which they were offered for sale are on average about €670 below the prices of cars that were registered in the same year as they were offered for sale. Further, the additional depreciation of cars that were registered earlier than one year prior to the advertisement year is on average about €641, etc. Therefore, these price discontinuities describe the average price difference between a car that was initially registered in January and a car that was initially registered one month earlier (December of the previous year). The price drops range from approximately €300 to €700 and are on average higher for newer cars. Noticeably, the price drops are even very high for relatively old cars. This is plausible because the older a car the more insufficient is the attention to the exact age of a car and only the year of the first registration becomes a relevant factor for the car valuation. These results support the findings of Englmaier et al. (2017). Moreover, they obtained findings show that price discontinuities exist in

---

[103]See also Appendix 4.7.3 for regression analysis with discontinuity design.

Table 4.6: **The Price Effect of Vintage Discontinuities on Used Cars**
This table lists the results of OLS regressions with robust standard errors. Regressions with discontinuities design is used by implementing dummy variables for each vintage threshold. Regression (A.1) only controls for a 6th order age polynomial, regression (A.2) adds control variables for mileage, power and engine type, regression (A.3) additionally incorporates the car model and the seller type and regression (A.4) considers the time when the advertisement was placed on the website of AutoScout24. The symbols †,*,**,*** indicate statistical significance at the 10%, 5%, 1% and 0.1% level, respectively.

	(A.1)	(A.2)	(A.3)	(A.4)
From the time of the advertisement: Registration earlier than ...				
...the advertisement year	178.292***	-121.603***	-278.649***	-670.218***
	(28.138)	(14.317)	(10.828)	(11.576)
...one year previously	-341.524***	-586.878***	-294.344***	-641.085***
	(30.864)	(14.472)	(10.269)	(10.98)
...two years previously	125.585***	-50.429**	-197.467***	-592.159***
	(33.779)	(15.651)	(10.66)	(11.225)
...three years previously	-421.730***	-243.418***	-299.114***	-658.155***
	(20.696)	(10.834)	(7.645)	(8.524)
...four years previously	-400.132***	-347.963***	-319.870***	-684.469***
	(21.573)	(13.078)	(9.765)	(10.443)
...five years previously	-501.570***	-384.984***	-245.356***	-614.013***
	(24.516)	(16.181)	(12.313)	(12.85)
...six years previously	-321.432***	-257.164***	-205.308***	-573.781***
	(23.66)	(17.476)	(13.237)	(13.741)
...seven years previously	-272.886***	-116.690***	-195.107***	-551.248***
	(23.626)	(19.39)	(14.757)	(15.253)
...eight years previously	-267.694***	34.768†	-64.910***	-431.205***
	(24.172)	(20.778)	(16.048)	(16.536)
...nine years previously	-335.017***	41.891†	-95.178***	-445.334***
	(24.954)	(22.047)	(17.364)	(17.818)
...ten years previously	-461.395***	159.535***	49.826**	-297.590***
	(22.359)	(22.639)	(18.208)	(18.656)
...eleven years previously	-319.253***	-66.498**	-94.528***	-449.620***
	(23.49)	(25.503)	(20.604)	(20.983)
...twelve years previously	-322.174***	-150.508***	-137.915***	-467.572***
	(29.461)	(28.851)	(23.409)	(23.748)
...thirteen years previously	-204.179***	-254.839***	-192.049***	-519.291***
	(36.291)	(34.907)	(28.639)	(28.915)
...fourteen years previously	-356.775***	85.150†	-10.19	-359.173***
	(47.224)	(48.528)	(40.498)	(40.731)
6th order age polynomial	Yes	Yes	Yes	Yes
Controls for car characteristics		Yes	Yes	Yes
Car fixed effects			Yes	Yes
Time fixed effects				Yes
Constant	26138.640***	12690.782***	21580.271***	21714.462***
	(23.436)	(32.52)	(217.871)	(220.573)
Observations	6,922,846	6,922,846	6,922,846	6,922,846
R^2	0.28	0.786	0.883	0.883
Adjusted R^2	0.28	0.786	0.883	0.883

the entire used-car market as all available car models are incorporated and in contrast to
Englmaier et al. (2017) that they are even significant for all vintages.

Several robustness checks to confirm the findings regarding price discontinuities in the
used-car market are implemented. First, the regression analysis of Table 4.6 is repeated using logarithmized asking prices. The results are listed in Table 4.7 and verify the
obtained findings about significant price drops at each vintage threshold. An average
price drop at vintage thresholds in a range of around 2 to 8 percentage points can be
observed. The relative extent of the price drops is higher for old cars, which supports the
presumption that individuals' attention to the exact car age decreases the older a car is.

To further verify the robustness of the obtained results, the order of the age polynomial
is varied as proposed by Lee and Lemieux (2010) and Englmaier et al. (2017). As the
correct functional form, which determines the relationship between the price and the age
of a car, is unknown and not ascertainable, the results should at least be consistent to
polynomial functions of the car age of higher and lower order. The regression results are
presented in Table 4.8.

Although some small changes of the extent of the price drops can be found at vintage
thresholds by varying the order of the age polynomial, all coefficients are still negative
and highly significant. The results are therefore robust to varying the order of the age
polynomial.

In the next step, it is analyzed if the price discontinuities could be a result of a left-
digit bias in the evaluation of the real car age similar to the price drops at 10,000 miles
threshold as described by Lacetera et al. (2012). This would imply that the price drops
exist although individuals take the actual age of a car into account in their pricing process
and not only the car vintage but are mistaken by concentrating on the left-most digit of
the car age. As the real car age is not directly reported in the advertisements, it can be
assumed that there should not be any price effects observable at an age threshold (1-year
old, 2-years old, etc.). This would support that the price evaluation of cars is based on the

Table 4.7: **Robustness Check - Vintage Discontinuities: Logarithmized Prices**
This table lists the results of OLS regressions with robust standard errors
employing logarithmized asking prices as dependent variable. Regression
analyses with discontinuities design are used and dummy variables are implemented for each vintage threshold. Regression (B.1) only controls for 8th order age polynomial, regression (B.2) adds control variables for mileage, power and engine type, regression (B.3) additionally incorporates the car model
and the seller type and regression (B.4) considers the time when the advertisement was placed on the website of AutoScout24. The symbols †,*,**,***
indicate statistical significance at the 10%, 5%, 1% and 0.1% level, respectively.

	(B.1)	(B.2)	(B.3)	(B.4)
From the time of the advertisement: Registration earlier than ...				
...the advertisement year	0.013***	-0.006***	-0.015***	-0.035***
	(0.001)	(0.000)	(0.000)	(0.000)
...one year previously	-0.018***	-0.024***	-0.008***	-0.026***
	(0.001)	(0.001)	(0.000)	(0.000)
...two years previously	0.047***	0.014***	-0.003***	-0.023***
	(0.001)	(0.001)	(0.000)	(0.000)
...three years previously	-0.010***	-0.011***	-0.017***	-0.034***
	(0.001)	(0.001)	(0.000)	(0.000)
...four years previously	-0.033***	-0.030***	-0.023***	-0.042***
	(0.001)	(0.001)	(0.000)	(0.000)
...five years previously	-0.042***	-0.033***	-0.023***	-0.042***
	(0.001)	(0.001)	(0.001)	(0.001)
...six years previously	-0.022***	-0.016***	-0.021***	-0.040***
	(0.002)	(0.001)	(0.001)	(0.001)
...seven years previously	-0.018***	-0.010***	-0.021***	-0.040***
	(0.002)	(0.001)	(0.001)	(0.001)
...eight years previously	-0.027***	-0.013***	-0.020***	-0.039***
	(0.002)	(0.001)	(0.001)	(0.001)
...nine years previously	-0.045***	-0.030***	-0.034***	-0.051***
	(0.002)	(0.002)	(0.001)	(0.001)
...ten years previously	-0.095***	-0.059***	-0.049***	-0.066***
	(0.003)	(0.002)	(0.001)	(0.001)
...eleven years previously	-0.078***	-0.060***	-0.054***	-0.072***
	(0.003)	(0.002)	(0.002)	(0.002)
...twelve years previously	-0.078***	-0.060***	-0.057***	-0.075***
	(0.004)	(0.003)	(0.002)	(0.002)
...thirteen years previously	-0.031***	-0.029***	-0.037***	-0.055***
	(0.005)	(0.003)	(0.003)	(0.003)
...fourteen years previously	-0.088***	-0.072***	-0.059***	-0.077***
	(0.006)	(0.005)	(0.004)	(0.004)
8th order age polynomial	Yes	Yes	Yes	Yes
Controls for car characteristics		Yes	Yes	Yes
Car fixed effects			Yes	Yes
Time fixed effects				Yes
Constant	10.012***	8.718***	9.157***	9.165***
	(0.001)	(0.001)	(0.045)	(0.045)
Observations	6,922,846	6,922,846	6,922,846	6,922,846
R^2	0.587	0.88	0.938	0.938
Adjusted R^2	0.587	0.88	0.938	0.938

Table 4.8: **Robustness Check - Varying the Order of the Age Polynomial**
This table lists the results of OLS regressions with robust standard errors for the data set of nearly seven million used-car advertisements of an Internet platform. Regressions with discontinuities design are used and dummy variables are implemented for each vintage threshold. Regression (C.1) - (C.5) use all available car information as control variables and differ only in varying the order (4 to 8) of the age polynomial. The symbols †,*,**,*** indicate statistical significance at the 10%, 5%, 1% and 0.1% level, respectively.

	(C.1)	(C.2)	(C.3)	(C.4)	(C.5)
From the time of the advertisement: Registration earlier than ...					
...the advertisement year	-680.879***	-661.256***	-670.218***	-677.295***	-677.295***
	(11.089)	(11.411)	(11.619)	(11.619)	(11.619)
...one year previously	-641.513***	-667.014***	-641.085***	-600.103***	-600.103***
	(10.433)	(10.464)	(10.98)	(11.581)	(11.581)
...two years previously	-564.566***	-612.948***	-592.159***	-599.811***	-599.811***
	(9.758)	(10.624)	(11.225)	(11.166)	(11.166)
...three years previously	-630.374***	-648.939***	-658.155***	-696.232***	-696.232***
	(8.347)	(8.557)	(8.524)	(8.753)	(8.753)
...four years previously	-668.281***	-658.255***	-684.469***	-708.364***	-708.364***
	(9.987)	(9.993)	(10.443)	(10.586)	(10.586)
...five years previously	-632.474***	-589.015***	-614.013***	-584.929***	-584.929***
	(11.797)	(12.399)	(12.85)	(13.016)	(13.016)
...six years previously	-628.432***	-571.891***	-573.781***	-507.735***	-507.735***
	(12.743)	(13.736)	(13.741)	(14.598)	(14.598)
...seven years previously	-626.325***	-577.081***	-551.248***	-495.521***	-495.521***
	(14.111)	(14.851)	(15.253)	(15.865)	(15.865)
...eight years previously	-494.526***	-474.026***	-431.205***	-431.671***	-431.671***
	(15.365)	(15.48)	(16.536)	(16.536)	(16.536)
...nine years previously	-462.326***	-483.817***	-445.334***	-511.394***	-511.394***
	(16.85)	(16.987)	(17.818)	(18.555)	(18.555)
...ten years previously	-243.586***	-305.497***	-297.590***	-382.634***	-382.634***
	(17.632)	(18.626)	(18.656)	(19.786)	(19.786)
...eleven years previously	-328.287***	-413.019***	-449.620***	-475.624***	-475.624***
	(18.701)	(20.344)	(20.983)	(21.05)	(21.05)
...twelve years previously	-338.700***	-401.850***	-467.572***	-379.490***	-379.490***
	(21.317)	(22.034)	(23.748)	(24.777)	(24.777)
...thirteen years previously	-531.741***	-496.090***	-519.291***	-415.591***	-415.591***
	(28.513)	(28.827)	(28.915)	(29.961)	(29.961)
...fourteen years previously	-569.040***	-435.575***	-359.173***	-461.766***	-461.766***
	(36.21)	(38.87)	(40.731)	(41.785)	(41.785)
Order of age polynomial	4th	5th	6th	7th	8th
Controls for car characteristics	Yes	Yes	Yes	Yes	Yes
Car fixed effects	Yes	Yes	Yes	Yes	Yes
Time fixed effects	Yes	Yes	Yes	Yes	Yes
Constant	21683.509***	21719.923***	21714.462***	21671.262***	21671.262***
	(221.223)	(220.872)	(220.573)	(221.324)	(221.324)
Observations	6,922,846	6,922,846	6,922,846	6,922,846	6,922,846
R^2	0.883	0.883	0.883	0.883	0.883
Adjusted R^2	0.883	0.883	0.883	0.883	0.883

initial registration year and not on the actual age of a car. Table 4.9 lists the regression results using dummy variables as indicators if a car is older than an age threshold.

Again, several control variables are included successively. The results of regression (D.4) support the presumption that crossing an age threshold does not affect the used-car prices significantly. Although some significant coefficients can be found, the price effect is not significant for most dummy variables. Moreover, the significant coefficients are positive except for the dummy variable that indicates if a car is older than one year, which is not in line with the price drops at vintage thresholds and seems not plausible. The significant positive coefficients for cars older than ten and eleven years can be explained by a small number of observations for old cars in the observed data set, [104] leading to less heterogeneity within this car segment, as well as positive price effects for these old cars due to a supply shock caused by the German scrappage premium. [105] It can therefore be rejected that the price discontinuities in the used-car market are a result of a left-digit bias at the evaluation of the exact car age. This is reasonable because potential car buyers and sellers have to calculate the car age on their own as the difference of the actual date and the date of the initial registration. A left-digit bias would require that the car age is directly observable, which is not listed in online used-car markets in general.

The previous results give evidence that the pricing of a used car is based on the year of the initial registration additionally to the actual age of the car. As an explanation of the observed price discontinuities, it is expected that the used-car pricing is based on the prices of cars which were registered in the middle of a year (maybe June and July), which represent the average car value of a vintage. An implication of this assumption is that cars which were initially registered in the first half of a year and which are older than the other cars of that registration year might be offered for sale by a higher price than their adequate car value and therefore might be overvalued and cars which were initially registered in the second half of a year might be undervalued as they are newer than the

---

[104] Only 2.8% of all advertisements are cars which are ten years old and 2.4% of all advertisements belong to cars which are eleven years old.

[105] See Chapter 5 and Gürtler et al. (2016). Gürtler et al. (2016) show that the average price of old used cars increased due to a supply shock caused by the scrappage of nearly two million clunkers in the year 2009 if their values are below the scrappage premium of €2,500. They determine that this was true for cars, which were about eleven years old.

Table 4.9: **Robustness Check - Age Thresholds**
This table lists the results of OLS regressions with robust standard errors for the data set of nearly seven million used-car advertisements of an Internet platform. Regressions with discontinuities design are used and dummy variables are implemented for each age threshold. Regression (D.1) only controls for a 6th order age polynomial, regression (D.2) adds control variables for mileage, power and engine type, regression (D.3) additionally incorporates the model and the seller type and regression (D.4) considers the time when the advertisement was placed on the website of AutoScout24. The symbols †,*,**,*** indicate statistical significance at the 10%, 5%, 1% and 0.1% level, respectively.

	(D.1)	(D.2)	(D.3)	(D.4)
Car older than ...				
... one year	-116.368***	-269.402***	-71.734***	-47.790***
	(30.139)	(14.579)	(10.709)	(10.681)
... two years	226.592***	196.039***	123.609***	96.695***
	(43.651)	(20.236)	(13.852)	(13.772)
... three years	233.907***	289.810***	13.837	-14.683
	(28.857)	(13.927)	(9.573)	(9.493)
... four years	19.484	187.179***	26.721*	24.285*
	(25.106)	(14.431)	(10.44)	(10.401)
... five years	-196.249***	-119.426***	18.306	15.258
	(28.37)	(17.776)	(13.382)	(13.351)
... six years	-18.239	-99.374***	3.181	0.666
	(29.153)	(19.811)	(15.053)	(15.034)
... seven years	86.301**	-74.721***	-7.981	-4.365
	(27.308)	(21.215)	(16.041)	(16.052)
... eight years	11.884	52.297*	42.110*	39.343*
	(28.055)	(23.762)	(18.188)	(18.225)
... nine years	75.546*	104.048***	38.752*	25.505
	(29.803)	(25.303)	(19.525)	(19.57)
... ten years	-136.773***	132.263***	65.407**	62.869**
	(29.051)	(26.29)	(20.798)	(20.861)
... eleven years	-107.016***	133.316***	133.596***	110.423***
	(27.211)	(27.802)	(22.271)	(22.342)
... twelve years	-74.526*	-28.954	-6.498	-11.189
	(31.737)	(32.635)	(26.459)	(26.524)
... thirteen years	14.512	-180.596***	-29.092	-13.911
	(39.502)	(36.66)	(29.635)	(29.708)
... fourteen years	-34.457	-53.81	-10.076	-8.239
	(51.661)	(49.362)	(40.786)	(40.849)
6th order age polynomial	Yes	Yes	Yes	Yes
Controls for car characteristics		Yes	Yes	Yes
Car fixed effects			Yes	Yes
Time fixed effects				Yes
Constant	26102.398***	12635.526***	21554.715***	21649.595***
	(24.486)	(32.698)	(217.884)	(219.132)
Observations	6,922,846	6,922,846	6,922,846	6,922,846
R^2	0.28	0.786	0.883	0.883
Adjusted R^2	0.28	0.786	0.883	0.883

average car of the same registration year. Consequently, the absolute price discrepancy must be greater the higher the age difference to the basis months June and July of the same year is. For this reason, it is not sufficient to investigate the annual price effect of a registration year, but the within-year price effect must be examined.

4.7.3 Regression with Discontinuity Design

Regression with a discontinuity design is a statistical approach to identify the causal effects of a treatment using a discontinuity in the control variable. For this purpose, a threshold is assigned above or below the occurrence of the treatment. In the case that the treatment status is a deterministic and discontinuous functions of an explanatory variable x_i the sharp regression discontinuity is used, which models this discontinuity by

$$D_i = \begin{cases} 1 & if \ x_i \geq c \\ 0 & if \ x_i < c \end{cases} \tag{4.7}$$

where c is the known threshold.[106] This results in the following regression model:

$$y = \beta_0 + \beta_D D + \beta_x x + u, \tag{4.8}$$

where y is the dependent variable, x contains the explanatory variable, u is the error term, β_x the coefficient of the variable x and β_0 constant. β_D is the causal effect of interest.

---

[106]See Angrist and Pischke (2009, p. 251 ff.).

5 The Price Effect of Supply and Demand Shocks on Secondary Markets

5.1 Fundamentals and Research Questions

In this chapter, the effect of competition between primary and secondary markets of durable goods, the price effect of supply and demand shocks caused by government interventions on secondary markets, and the functioning and price-formation process on secondary markets with heterogeneous agents are striven to explain. Durable goods industries are frequently characterized by decentralized secondary markets, in which used products are traded without the direct control of manufacturers of new goods. The automotive sector is the most prominent example of this market structure. According to the National Independent Automobile Dealers Association, more than 15.5 million new vehicles and nearly 42 million used vehicles were sold in the United States in 2013, whereas approximately 2.9 million new vehicles and 7.1 million used vehicles were sold in Germany in the same year.[107] The deterioration of the quality of durable goods over time and the preference for a better quality of previously owned cars by consumers due to technological progress generate trading in the secondary market.

---

[107]See Federal Motor Transport Authority (2017b) and Federal Motor Transport Authority (2017a).

Against this background, the effect of governmental interventions that are introduced to strengthen the profitability of primary markets on secondary markets is analyzed. For this purpose, the following research questions is answered using the example of the used-car market:

- What is the price effect of supply and demand shocks caused by governmental interventions on secondary markets?
- How does sellers' level of information and experience affect their used-car pricing after these shocks?

Based on two data sets, the effect of the German accelerated vehicle retirement program on used-car prices in the secondary market is empirically analyzed. These data sets consist of sales prices from a leasing company and from an Internet platform for used cars. Whereas the average price reaction to the accelerated vehicle retirement program is modest, it can be shown that some car segments are strongly affected by the subsidy. First, a significant decline in prices of small young cars during the subsidy period (short-run effect) is observed and it is found out that the medium-run effect of the price reactions is even greater. This price decline is the consequence of a reduced demand for used cars of low mileage because the substitutability by new subsidized cars is particularly high for the segment of small young cars. Second, it is found out that prices for old clunkers, whose price is less than the scrappage premium, significantly increased during the scrappage scheme and that these higher prices remain at the end of the subsidy. This price increase is a consequence of a decreased supply of these old vehicles in the secondary market due to the scrappage of old clunkers. Hence, the average price effect for the entire used-car market may be neutralized or just small, but it is substantial for different car segments. Third, a different pricing behavior of professional car dealers and households after implementation of the accelerated vehicle retirement program is detected. Car dealers react more rapidly to developments in the used-car market due to better customer contacts and experience, which gives evidence for information asymmetries in the used-car market.

The relevance of this investigations is manifold. Accelerated vehicle retirement programs were launched by many countries in reaction to the financial crisis of 2007-08 and are frequently employed as political instruments for stimulating the economy. Topics such as air pollution and road safety will be contemporary issues in the future. Thus, it is likely that scrappage premiums will be applied by governments. For an impact assessment of such scrappage premiums, it is crucial to understand not only the sales effects on the primary market but also the price effects on the secondary market. Furthermore, leasing companies and auto banks, which are exposed to the residual value risk of their leasing agreements, are very interested in the extent of political interventions such as scrappage schemes because they have to adjust their risk management and predictions of future residual values to cover their risk. In addition, car manufactures have increased their focus on the used-car market in the last several years due to sluggish new-car registrations and a high demand for second-hand cars. Therefore, an accurate evaluation of the effect of accelerated vehicle retirement programs on the entire automobile market has significant political and entrepreneurial relevance. Finally, the results of this analysis allow insights into the general functioning and price reactions on secondary markets after supply and demand shocks, for example, due to government subsidies and scrappage programs. The established empirical analysis, the theoretical conception and the findings of this chapter are based on a paper written by Gürtler et al. (2016).

This chapter proceeds as follows: In the next section, a literature overview about the effects of governmental subsidies on the primary and secondary market is given. Section 5.3 provides a short overview about the German scrappage scheme in 2009. In Section 5.4.2, a simple model to derive the analyzed hypotheses is introduced. Section 5.5 starts with a description of the German automobile market and introduces the data sets for the regression analyses. Subsequently, the empirical strategy and the empirical study are presented in Section 5.5.2 and Section 5.6, respectively. Robustness checks are provided in Section 5.7. Section 5.8 offers some concluding remarks.

5.2 Literature Review

Next, a literature review of studies focusing on the interaction between the primary and the secondary market and the effect of governmental intervention, such as subsidies and accelerated vehicle retirement programs on both markets will be given.

Existing studies have modeled the interactions between demand behavior and supply behavior in the primary and secondary markets by discrete choice models, which provide implicit information about price changes in the automobile market (Schiraldi, 2011; Adda and Cooper, 2000). However, this modeling was performed for the entire used-car market; different price levels or car segments were not analyzed. Whereas the overall price reaction may be negligible, the prices of some car segments may be substantially affected by changes in demand and supply. Thus, there is a lack of knowledge how secondary market prices of different car segments react to supply and demand shocks that are caused by government interventions.[108]

There exist several related streams in the literature. A first stream investigates the competitiveness of the secondary market. Chen et al. (2013) investigate whether active secondary markets aid or harm durable goods manufacturers. Using a dynamic equilibrium model, they show that the opening of secondary markets decreases profits for manufacturers of new and durable goods. For certain conditions, they also reveal an increase in profitability due to the opening of secondary markets. Esteban and Shum (2007) confirm the competitive importance of secondary markets. However, both studies only consider the effect of competition on the manufacture of new durable goods and do not evaluate the implications for secondary markets. Gavazza et al. (2014) investigate the allocative and welfare effect of secondary markets for cars. They discover that aggregate effects on consumer surplus and welfare are relatively small and that low-income households may experience a significant decrease in welfare. Price effects are not analyzed in their study.

---

[108]Busse et al. (2012) analyzed the price effect of scrappage schemes on very old clunkers, which was caused by a supply shortage. However, they could not identify any price changes, which may be attributed to the neglected differentiation between car classifications.

Other studies analyze the effect of governmental interaction on the automobile market with focus on new-car sales and manufacturer benefits. Chen et al. (2010) analyze the stimulating effect of tax credits and determine that the benefit of reducing the sales tax decreases with the durability of the product. Mitra and Webster (2008) discover a competitive behavior between a manufacturer and a remanufacturer in a two-period model and emphasize that government subsidies should be shared among market participants to increase their profits. Other papers explore the effect of equipment investments and government subsidies on economic growth and the supply of goods (De Long and Summers, 1991; Andreoni and Bergstrom, 1996; Bergström, 2000) but do not focus on secondary markets.

Another related stream of literature analyzes the sales effects of accelerated vehicle retirement programs. Based on a discrete choice model, Adda and Cooper (2000) and Schiraldi (2011) evaluate the short- and long-run effects of the French and Italian scrappage schemes. They found that the number of sales increased immediately after the start of the program; these sales were offset in the long-run. Similar results were obtained by Li et al. (2013), Mian and Sufi (2012) and Hoekstra et al. (2017) for the 'cash-for-clunkers' program in the United States. Using a difference-in-differences approach, Grigolon et al. (2016) show that scrappage programs prevented total sales reductions for the European automobile market. Müller and Heimeshoff (2013) confirm this result and observe a positive total effect of the incentives in the United States, South Korea, Germany and the United Kingdom. Positive short-run sales effects are observed by Cantos-Sánchez et al. (2018) for the Spanish automobile market and a neutral effect of financial aid on Spanish household welfare. However, the focus of these studies is to measure the total effect on the sales results in the primary market; they do not consider the price effect on the secondary market or distinguish between different car segments.

The German scrappage scheme, which is the focus of this empirical study, has also been investigated in the literature. Böckers et al. (2012) observe increasing demand for new small cars during the time of the subsidy and low or immeasurable pull-forward effects. Other studies analyze spillover effects and linkages to other branches of industries because the savings from car purchases can be applied to the consumption of other goods (Haugh et al., 2010; Pfeifer, 2013). Moreover, some studies address the optimal design and effectiveness of accelerated vehicle retirement programs (Hahn, 1995; Alberini et al., 1995; Kavalec and Setiawan, 1997; Esteban, 2007) with a focus on the derivation of an optimal scrapping incentive or on the construction of a cost-efficient scheme in terms of emissions reductions.

This study contributes to the literature on the effect of government subsidies and scrappage scheme evaluations. Few studies evaluate the price effect of accelerated vehicle retirement programs, especially on the secondary market. Studies primarily consider prices in the primary market and analyze how the rebate benefited consumers (Kaul et al., 2012; Witte, 2013; Busse et al., 2012). The investigation of Busse et al. (2012) considers price changes in the secondary market. However, they only focus on price levels of old low-cost used cars that suffer from conditional offer caused by high scrappage rates during the subsidy; they do not address the price effect on the entire used-car market. Their results differ from the findings of this study, which may be attributed to neglected differentiation in terms of car classifications. This analysis of the German scrappage scheme investigates price shocks that are caused by this government subsidy to the secondary market in the short-run and medium-run and considers different car segments. Although Böckers et al. (2012) consider different car classifications they only investigate the implications for new-car sales. Moreover, this study contributes to the welfare evaluation of scrappage schemes. The findings obtained suggest that not only the effect on the primary market but also the welfare losses on the secondary market should be considered when evaluating the welfare effects of a subsidy, which are produced by the decreasing demand for young used cars and an insufficient supply of old cars for low-income households. Based on these results, it can be deduced that low-income households experienced significant welfare losses as a consequence of the scrappage program, which is consistent with the theoretical analysis of Gavazza et al. (2014). This empirical study provides evidence for information asymmetries in the used-car market.

5.3 Germany's Scrappage Scheme

As a response to the financial crisis of 2007-08 and the continuing slowdown in the economy in the third quarter of 2008, the German government implemented many programs to stimulate the German economy. One reaction to the crisis was an accelerated vehicle retirement program, which was a very popular scheme among many developed countries at this time. Notably, all members of the G8, China and many other countries, especially members of the OECD, launched similar programs.[109] These schemes subsidized consumers and car manufacturers for purchasing a new car and scrapping an old fuel-inefficient clunker. Other designs of accelerated vehicle retirement programs exist, in which only the scrappage of old gas-guzzling vehicles is subsidized; however, the German scrappage scheme directly supports automobile manufacturers.[110] The incentive of the scrappage premium was to increase the demand for new cars and stabilize the German automobile industry, which is frequently referred to as the backbone of the German economy. Linkages to other industries and supply firms should trigger a multiplier effect on the total economy. Haugh et al. (2010) observed that an increase in output of the automobile production in the G7 countries generated an output that was three times the total production in these countries. Pfeifer (2013) also measures spillover effects on other industrial sectors because subsidized households, which received scrappage bonuses, spent more money on other consumption goods. Scrapping gas-guzzling vehicles and replacing them with new fuel-efficient cars should also reduce carbon dioxide emissions and improve road safety.[111]

Immediately after the announcement by Vice-Chancellor Frank-Walter Steinmeier on December 27, 2008, the German government implemented an accelerated vehicle retirement program on January 14, 2009, which subsidized households with a premium of €2,500 for replacing an old car with a new car. Commercial automobile purchases were

---

[109]Refer to Witte (2013) and Pfeifer (2013) for a detailed overview of the scrappage scheme in Germany and the accelerated vehicle retirement programs of other countries.

[110]Refer to Schiraldi (2011), Esteban (2007), and Kavalec and Setiawan (1997) for 'cash-for-scrappage' schemes without replacement.

[111]Alberini et al. (1996), Van Wee et al. (2000), Dill (2004), Knittel (2009), Li et al. (2013) and Lenski et al. (2010) analyzed the environmental effects of 'cash-for-clunkers' programs and observed a positive effect of scrappage programs on emissions reductions.

not eligible for the program. To receive a bonus, the old vehicle had to be older than nine years and registered with the applicant for a minimum of one year. Thus, receiving a premium by buying an old clunker immediately before buying a new car was not possible. The replacement car had to be a new or used vehicle that was not older than 14 months (employee's car). The car had to comply with the emissions standard Euro 4, which had already become a standard attribute for new cars in Germany at this time. An overview of the requirements of the German scrappage scheme and guidelines are published by the Federal Office of Economics and Export Control Federal Office of Economics and Export Control (2009).

First, the budget of this scrapping scheme was set to €1.5 billion; however, significant demand caused a rapid decrease in monetary resources from this budget. As a result the German government increased the budget to €5 billion at the end of March 2009. The budget of the German scrappage scheme had a proportion of more than half of all funds of the countries of the European Union and a third of the worldwide budget for accelerated vehicle retirement programs at that time (Witte, 2013). Therefore, the German scrappage scheme became the most eligible candidate when analyzing the effect of 'cash-for-clunkers' program on automobile markets and of exogenous supply and demand shocks on secondary markets of durable goods. Despite this extremely large budget, the German scrappage program was exhausted in September 2009 prior to the established expiration period at the end of 2009.

As a result of this financial incentive to purchase a new car, registrations of new cars increased in 2009. Figure 5.1 presents the development of monthly registrations between 2007 and 2011 for the entire primary market and distinguishes between private car sales and commercial car sales from 2008 to 2010. The high number of registrations in 2009 was driven by private not commercial sales. This emphasizes the success of the program because the large sales in 2009 were induced by the scrappage subsidy. [112]

---

[112] The scrappage program was subject of intense discussions in the media, so that most households have very likely been aware of the scrappage premium. This is confirmed by the fact that the budget was exhausted prior to the established expiration date.

Figure 5.1: **Monthly New-Car Registrations in Germany (2007-2011)**
Source: Federal Motor Transport Authority (2012).

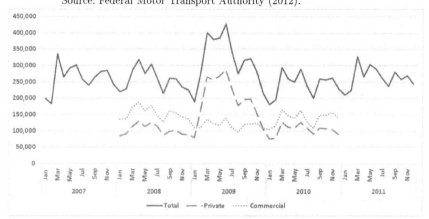

After the program's budget was exhausted, the quantity sold approximately falls back to the normal level (Q4/2009). However, not all subsidized cars were already registered during the premium period. Because of the high numbers of sales closures in the second and third quarter in 2009, production bottlenecks of car manufacturers causes delayed new-car registrations. Hence, in contrast to Figure 5.1, new-car sales may be lower after the program's budget was exhausted than before the scrappage scheme as a possible result of pull-forward effects.

As previously mentioned, some studies analyze the effect of the German scrappage scheme on total car sales in the primary market during the subsidy period and the long-term effect considering the periods subsequent to the scrappage period. Müller and Heimeshoff (2013) observe positive sales effects even when the period after the subsidy is considered. This result is confirmed by Böckers et al. (2012), who stated that approximately one million additional cars were registered in 2009 compared with the counterfactual situation.

As shown in Figure 5.1, new car registrations increased during the subsidy period in 2009. Sales increased from 3.1 million in 2008 to more than 3.8 million in 2009, as reported

Figure 5.2: **Monthly New-Car Registrations in Germany for Different Car Classifications (2008-2011)**
Source: Federal Motor Transport Authority (2012).

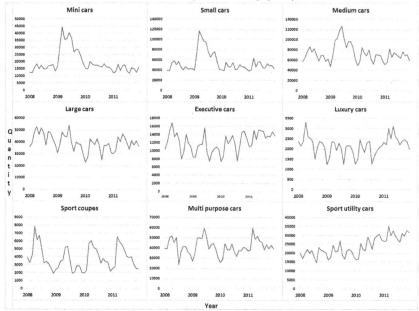

by the Federal Motor Transport Authority. However, the total number of subsidized vehicles was two million, which indicates that the windfall gains of car holders, who would have purchased a new car anyway, diminish the success of the program. When examining the distribution of the new-car registrations, a relevant increase in demand is only evident for the smaller car segments (see Figure 5.2). The registrations of mini cars increased by more than 100%, small car registrations increased by more than 50% and medium cars increased by nearly 30%, whereas the remaining segments did not show any recognizable changes. Thus, it seems that only the registrations of low-priced vehicles were affected by the scrappage scheme, which is consistent with the findings of Böckers et al. (2012), whereas the sales of the remaining segments did not change.[113] The effect may be significantly higher than the reported percentages because the poor economic situation in a scenario without a scrappage scheme may have caused decreasing numbers of sales in 2009 compared with the previous year.

According to Böckers et al. (2012), pull-forward effects reduced the sales of small cars in 2010 and 2011 by approximately 40,000 which are small compared with the surplus in 2009. In Figure 5.2, the new-car registrations in the following year provide an indication of the lower demand in these segments even if the effect is rather small.

5.4 Modeling Approach and Hypotheses

In this section, several hypotheses about the effect of the scrappage premium on used-car prices are derived, which will be tested in Section 5.6. In the first step, a theoretical model is implemented, which describes consumers' choice regarding the purchase of a car from the set of all new and used cars that are attainable in the primary and secondary market (see Section 5.4.1). Using this model, the immediate impact of the introduction of the scrappage premium on supply and demand will be explained and hypotheses about the resulting price effect for used cars in the following periods will be derived (see Section 5.4.2).

5.4.1 Model

Let N_t be the set of all new and used cars that are attainable in the primary and secondary market at time t. Following Schiraldi (2011), consumer i's net utility flow of car $j \in N_t$ at time t is modeled as

$$u_{i,j,k,t} = \hat{u}_i(q_{j,t}) - \alpha_i p_{j,t} + \alpha_i p_{k,t} + \epsilon_{i,j,t}, \ j \in N_t, \tag{5.1}$$

---

[113]Detailed information about new car registrations are published by the Federal Motor Transport Authority and are provided at http://www.kba.de/EN/Home/home_node.html; last accessed: December 31, 2018.

where $p_{j,t}$ denotes the price of car j at time t and $p_{k,t}$ corresponds to the value of consumer i's old car k. $\hat{u}_i(q_{j,t})$ is defined as consumer i's utility value of owning car j at time t, which depends on the car's quality level $q_{j,t}$. The quality value $q_{j,t}$ in turn is determined by the observed physical characteristics of car j at time t (for example mileage, age, fuel, model, etc.). As consumers' utility flow increases in the car's quality, $\hat{u}' > 0$. Assuming a diminishing marginal utility, it follows that $\hat{u}'' < 0$. Consumer i's preference parameter α_i describes the marginal utility from wealth, which is assumed to be constant, and $\epsilon_{i,j,t}$ is an error term with zero mean and constant variance, which is independent across consumers, products and time. For $j = k$ the net utility flow of consumer i equals the utility flow of retaining the old vehicle. For reasons of simplicity, transaction costs are neglected and it is assumed that consumer i will not use the outside option: selling his car without a replacement. Moreover, it is assumed that consumer i is the owner of a clunker k and entitled to the scrappage premium if he decides buying a new car and scrapping the old vehicle k at the same time.

In the following, let $j \in N_t = \{\text{new cars, used cars}\}$. For each car model it is assumed that the price of the new car exceeds the price of the used car and that the quality of the new car is favored over the quality of the old car, i.e. $p_{new,t} > p_{used,t}$ and $E(\hat{u}_i(q_{new,t})) > E(\hat{u}_i(q_{used,t}))$ for all t and i. Prior to the introduction of the scrappage scheme $(t = t_1)$, consumer i's expected net utility flow of a used car $(j = used)$ with quality value q_{used,t_1} is greater than the expected net utility flow of a new car $(j = new)$ with quality q_{new,t_1} if

$$\alpha_i > \frac{\hat{u}_i(q_{new,t_1}) - \hat{u}_i(q_{used,t_1})}{p_{new,t_1} - p_{used,t_1}} =: \alpha_{i,1}. \tag{5.2}$$

At the time of the introduction of the scrappage scheme $(t = t_2)$, consumer i will receive a premium of €2,500 if he decides to scrap his old clunker k and buy a new car $(j = new)$. In this case, consumer i will not receive the market value p_{k,t_2} of his clunker and he prefers to buy a used car instead of a new car if

$$\alpha_i > \frac{\hat{u}_i(q_{new,t_2}) - \hat{u}_i(q_{used,t_2})}{p_{new,t_2} + p_{k,t_2} - 2500 - p_{used,t_2}} =: \alpha_{i,2}. \tag{5.3}$$

To measure the immediate effect of the introduction of the scrappage scheme on supply and demand of used cars, it is assumed that price and quality of cars do not change between the period before the introduction of the scrappage scheme ($t = t_1$) and the time of the program's start ($t = t_2$). As the scrappage premium was announced shortly before the program's start, it can be expected that the supply side of cars is on a constant level. For this reason, the time index t is omitted in the following. It is assumed that the price of clunker k is below €2,500, which results in $\alpha_{i,2} > \alpha_{i,1}$ for all consumers i. This means that all consumers who have a marginal utility from wealth $\alpha_i \in (\alpha_{i,1}, \alpha_{i,2})$ would have purchased a used car without the implementation of the scrappage premium but because of the introduction of the scrappage scheme they buy a new car. As a consequence, the demand for used cars decreases during the time of the scrappage program.

Next, the influence of the car's quality on the extent of the interval $(\alpha_{i,1}, \alpha_{i,2})$ is analyzed. For simplicity, only used cars of the same age are considered and it is assumed that the quality is increasing in the seize of the car segment. In the following, the abbreviations $q := q_{new}$ and $p := p_{new}$ is used and the plausible assumption is made that the (absolute) price difference $p - p_{used}$ between new and used cars of the same type is strictly increasing in the quality level q. Furthermore, it is assumed for simplicity that an increase of the quality level is identical for new and used cars of the same type, i.e. $\partial q_{used}/\partial q = 1$. Under these conditions, the following theorem states that the extent of the interval $(\alpha_{i,1}, \alpha_{i,2})$ reduces if the quality level q increases.

Theorem 4.1. *Let $c := 2500 - p_k < p - p_{used}$, which means that the net premium of the scrappage bonus is smaller than the car's depreciation. Then, $\frac{\partial(\alpha_{i,2} - \alpha_{i,1})}{\partial q} < 0$, i.e., the extent of the interval $(\alpha_{i,1}, \alpha_{i,2})$ reduces if the quality q of the new car (and consequently the used car) increases.*

Proof. The statement of the theorem immediately follows because

$$
\begin{aligned}
\frac{\partial \alpha_{i,2}}{\partial q} &= \frac{\partial}{\partial q}\left(\frac{\hat{u}_i(q) - \hat{u}_i(q_{used})}{p - p_{used} - c}\right) \\
&= \frac{\hat{u}_i'(q) - \hat{u}_i'(q_{used})}{p - p_{used} - c} - \frac{(\hat{u}_i(q) - \hat{u}_i(q_{used})) \cdot \frac{\partial(p - p_{used})}{\partial q}}{(p - p_{used} - c)^2} \\
&< \frac{\hat{u}_i'(q) - \hat{u}_i'(q_{used})}{p - p_{used}} - \frac{(\hat{u}_i(q) - \hat{u}_i(q_{used})) \cdot \frac{\partial(p - p_{used})}{\partial q}}{(p - p_{used})^2} \\
&= \frac{\partial}{\partial q}\left(\frac{\hat{u}_i(q) - \hat{u}_i(q_{used})}{p - p_{used}}\right) = \frac{\partial \alpha_{i,1}}{\partial q}.
\end{aligned}
$$

The inequality in the second last line results because $\hat{u}_i$ is concave and consequently $\hat{u}_i'(q) - \hat{u}_i'(q_{used}) < 0$ and because $\partial(p - p_{used})/\partial q > 0$. $\qquad\square$

In the next section, the resulting secondary market price effects from these supply and demand shocks are considered in the following periods (after t_2).

5.4.2 Hypotheses

5.4.2.1 Model-based Hypotheses

According to equations (5.2) and (5.3), the demand for used-cars decreases after the implementation of the scrappage scheme because consumers that have a marginal utility from wealth $\alpha_i \in (\alpha_{i,1}, \alpha_{i,2})$ decided to buy a new car instead of an used car (preference without the scrappage premium). However, not all used-car segments are affected by the demand shock on the same extent. Consumers that have a marginal utility from wealth $\alpha_i > \alpha_{i,2}$ are buyers of old used cars most likely because of their small financial budgets. After the implementation of the scrappage premium, this consumer group will continue buying old used cars. Consumers that have a marginal utility from wealth $\alpha_i < \alpha_{i,1}$ are buyers of new cars. These results imply that a changing consumer behavior due to the scrappage scheme is not expected for this group, too. Only consumers that have a marginal utility from wealth $\alpha_i \in (\alpha_{i,1}, \alpha_{i,2})$ are influenced by the scrappage premium.

Before the program was introduced, this consumer group bought used cars and due to the scrappage scheme they switch to buy new cars. Thus, this group prefers cars of higher quality than consumers with $\alpha_i > \alpha_{i,2}$ and it seems to be plausible that this consumer group buys young used cars as long as no scrappage scheme was implemented. Hence, it can be expected that the demand effect of the implementation of the scrappage scheme is greatest for young used cars.

Adding the result of the Theorem 4.1, the interval $(\alpha_{i,1}, \alpha_{i,2})$ is rather small if the high quality car segment is considered and consequently, a price effect of the scrappage scheme for high quality cars cannot be expected. Instead, a price effect of the scrappage scheme for cars of the smaller segments is expected due to their low quality level. As a consequence of (5.2), (5.3) and Theorem 4.1, the price effect should be greatest for young used cars of the small(est) car segment. Thus, the following short-run demand shock hypothesis is derived:

> *Demand shock hypothesis (short-run) (H1a): The scrappage scheme causes a price decline for small young cars during the length of the scrappage program.*

The fixed bonus of €2,500 leads to a large percentage change of the new-car price whereas the relative effect for expensive cars is rather small. Given a similar price elasticity of demand for small and large cars, the response of the demanded quantity is substantially larger for small cars.[114]

In the next step, the medium-run effect of the scrappage premium on the prices of small and young used cars is considered. Similar to the derivation of equations (5.2) and (5.3), consumer i will not sell his clunker k and buy a car $j \in N_{t_1}$ at time t_1 (time without scrappage premium) if

$$\alpha_i > \frac{\hat{u}_i(q_{j,t_1}) - \hat{u}_i(q_{k,t_1})}{p_{j,t_1} - p_{k,t_1}} =: \alpha_{i,k,t_1}. \tag{5.4}$$

Instead, a part of this consumer group will sell their clunkers and buy a young and small used car in the following period. During the time of the scrappage premium (t_2),

---

[114]It has been shown that the absolute price elasticity of demand is relatively elastic for expensive goods such as new cars, but decreasing in the size of the car (Berry et al., 1995; Deng and Ma, 2010).

consumers preference changed because due to the scrappage premium only consumers that have a marginal utility from wealth

$$\alpha_i > \frac{\hat{u}_i(q_{j,t_2}) - \hat{u}_i(q_{k,t_2})}{p_{j,t_2} - 2500} =: \alpha_{i,k,t_2} \tag{5.5}$$

will not sell their clunker during the scrappage scheme. As by assumption $p_{k,t_2} < 2,500 \leq p_{j,t_2}$ for $j \neq k$, it follows that $\alpha_{i,k,t_1} < \alpha_{i,k,t_2}$ for all consumer i, clunker k and $j \neq k$. The obtained results imply, that the consumption behavior of consumers with $\alpha_i \geq \alpha_{i,k,t_2}$ is not affected by the scrappage premium. They will continue using their clunkers. The consumption behavior of consumers who have a marginal utility from wealth $\alpha_i \leq \alpha_{i,k,t_1}$ is not influenced by the scrappage premium as well. This consumer group would have sold their clunkers during the scrappage scheme anyway and some of the consumers can profit from windfall effects if they would buy a new car even in the case of no bonus. Consumers with $\alpha_i \in (\alpha_{i,k,t_1}, \alpha_{i,k,t_2})$ antedate their purchase decision and buy a new car during the scrappage scheme. Using the same argumentation as above, without the implementation of the scrappage program, some consumers of this group would have purchased a young and small used car in the following period, but because of the premium some of these consumers switch to buy a new car. Because of these pull-forward effects, it can be expected that the price decline of the small and low-mileage car segments continues after the budget of the scrappage scheme was exhausted. Hence, the following medium-run demand shock hypothesis is considered:

Demand shock hypothesis (medium-run) (H1b): The scrappage scheme causes a price decline for small young cars in the medium-run.

As shown by Böckers et al. (2012) and Müller and Heimeshoff (2013), a pull-forward effect decreased the demand for new cars in the period after the subsidy in Germany. People who considered buying a car within the next few years were incentivized by the scrappage bonus to pull their purchase decision forward.

A second result is that the supply of old used cars will decrease at time t_2 because all consumers with a marginal utility from wealth $\alpha_i \in (\alpha_{i,1}, \alpha_{i,2})$ decide to scrap their old vehicle instead of offering their clunker for sale in the secondary market. Hence, in addition to the vast sales of nearly two million new subsidized cars, the same amount of old clunkers left the used-car market. The demand for old cars should not be heavily affected by the scrappage scheme because only consumers with a preference parameter $\alpha_i \in (\alpha_{i,1}, \alpha_{i,2})$ changed their consumption behavior. As these consumers do not belong to the group of buyers of low-quality cars, the demand of clunkers should not be affected by the scrappage premium. Hence, an increase in the price of old clunkers is expected. Thus, the following short-run supply shock hypothesis is assumed:

Supply shock hypothesis (short-run) (H2a): Prices of old low-priced cars increase during the length of the scrappage subsidy.

A rational car holder who considers buying a new car will scrap his vehicle only if it is worth less than the scrappage bonus. This finding provides an indication of the high scrappage rates of cars from smaller segments because vehicles from the other segments are frequently more valuable than the scrappage premium even if they are older than nine years.[115] For this reason, a decline in the supply of cars of these segments is expected.

After the end of the scrappage scheme, a continued shortage of old clunkers in the secondary market is expected because the market requires several years until young vintage cars depreciate under the threshold of €2,500 and mitigate the enormous lack of old clunkers resulting from the used-car scrappage of consumers with $\alpha_i \in (\alpha_{i,1}, \alpha_{i,2})$ at the introduction of the scrappage premium. Additionally, clunkers of consumers with $\alpha_i \in (\alpha_{i,k,t_1}, \alpha_{i,k,t_2})$ that under normal circumstances would have entered the used-car market after the end of the scrappage program, left the market due to their scrappage. This leads to the following medium-run supply shock hypothesis:

Supply shock hypothesis (medium-run) (H2b): Prices of old low-priced cars increase after the introduction of the scrappage subsidy in the medium-run.

---

[115]From the two million scrapped cars generated by the subsidy, approximately 75% of the scrapped cars belonged to the segments of mini, small or medium cars (Federal Office of Economics and Export Control, 2010).

5.4.2.2 Further Hypotheses

Whereas hypothesis H1 and H2 refer to the overall price reaction for the segments of young and old cars, respectively, now possible differences between price offerings of private households versus car dealers for both car segments are considered. According to H1, decreasing prices for small young cars are assumed. For this car segment, significant differences in the price development for dealers' versus private offerings cannot be expected. Private car advertisements are assumed to be orientated based on dealers' prices, which are easily observable using the search function on Internet platforms. This indicates that the price-generation process of used cars is initiated by car dealers. For this reason the following transparency hypothesis is expected:

> *Transparency hypothesis (H3a): The price difference between a dealer and private advertisement for small young cars does not change due to the scrappage scheme.*

Conversely, the price adaption for car offerings of clunkers is less transparent for the following reasons: In contrast to the market of young cars, this market is not dominated by car dealers. Furthermore, the number of comparable advertisements for old clunkers is insufficient for directly matching a very old car, which somebody wants to sell, with an existing offering in the secondary market that is available on an Internet platform of used cars. In such a situation, car dealers have better abilities to assess market prices due to better possibilities to observe developments in the (non-transparent) secondary market and benefit from close customer contacts and their years of experience. Given the environment of increasing prices for old cars (according to hypothesis H2), car dealers can therefore benefit from their knowledge about the automobile market and can rapidly react to changes in demand and supply. Thus, at least in the medium-run, it is assumed that the prices of clunkers, which were offered by dealers, exhibited a greater increase than the prices of private offerings.

For this reason, the following information advantage hypothesis is expected:

> *Information advantage hypothesis (medium-run) (H3b): After the end of the scrappage scheme, the offering prices of old clunkers advertised by car dealers exhibited a greater increase than the prices of privately advertised clunkers.*

During the period of the scrappage premium (the 'short-run'), however, there exists an opposing effect. Only households had the option to buy a new car and receive €2,500 premium by scrapping their old cars. Because households want to be compensated for losing their premium option, the offering prices of privately-advertised old clunkers increased even further. Moreover, a household that decided to buy a new car would not have offered its clunker below €2,500 in the secondary market. Car dealers, though, did not have such an option. For this reason, it is possible that the prices of privately advertised old clunkers achieved a greater increase compared with prices of car dealers during the scrappage scheme. Even if this potentially means that private households found it difficult to sell their cars for the offered price in the secondary market, they still had the option of driving the car for a longer period. On the contrary, every day that a used car remains part of a dealer's stock, the car loses value without having a utility from using the car. If the effect from this option value was even greater than the (opposing) effect from hypothesis H3b, this results in the following supplier-specific option value hypotheses:

> *Option value hypothesis (short-run) (H3c): The offering prices of old clunkers, which were privately advertised during the scrappage scheme, exhibited a greater increase than the prices of clunkers, which were offered by dealers.*

If these hypotheses can be verified, it can be concluded that car dealers can benefit from information asymmetries mainly for old clunkers but not for young cars. According to hypothesis H3a, different price reaction in transparent markets are not expected. As soon as the market is less transparent and it becomes difficult for households to observe the prices of used cars, hypothesis H3b indicates that car dealers are more able to react to developments in the used-car market.

5.5 Data and Empirical Strategy

5.5.1 Description of the Data Set

After China, the United States and Japan, Germany has the fourth largest automobile market in the world. Without incorporating commercial vehicles, Germany ranks third after China and Japan. Approximately 5.7 million cars were produced in Germany in 2013, which rendered the automotive industry the most important industrial branch of this country compared with the sales of other industries.[116] In addition, Germans' automobile stock comprises more than 43 million passenger cars and more than 52 million motor vehicles, which emphasizes the importance of mobility in a country, where the average household has one car.[117] Figure 5.3 reports the new-car registrations and used-car sales in Germany from 2000 to 2013 as well as the corresponding sales value of these transactions during the same period.

Figure 5.3: **Yearly Registrations (Left) and Sales Value (Right) of New Cars and Used Cars in Germany**
Source: Federal Motor Transport Authority (2017b), Federal Motor Transport Authority (2017a) and Deutsche Automobil Treuhand (2016).

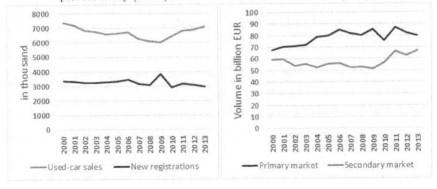

Every year, approximately 3 million new cars are sold in Germany, which produces a sales value of approximately €80 billion. Most cars are produced by the Volkswagen Group, which includes the marques Audi, Bentley, Bugatti, Lamborghini, Porsche, Seat, Skoda, Volkswagen and Volkswagen Commercial Vehicles. The Volkswagen Group has a market share of approximately 40% of all new registrations in Germany; with approximately 10.3 million sold cars in 2016, it is the largest car manufacturer in the world.

---

[116]Refer to http://www.oica.net; last accessed: December 31, 2018.
[117]Refer to Federal Motor Transport Authority, http://www.kba.de; last accessed: December 31, 2018.

However, the number of used-car transactions in the secondary market is significantly higher than the number of used-car transactions in the primary market. The Federal Motor Transport Authority referred to approximately 7 million used-car transactions in 2013 with a sales value of nearly €70 billion, which was slightly lower than the primary market sales value.[118] The significant importance of the German automobile market can be observed, which is dominated by vehicles of the Volkswagen Group. For this reason, the German automobile market, especially the market for cars of the Volkswagen Group, is highly relevant for an analysis of price reactions in the automobile market.

The data-base of this study consists of two different data sets of German used-car prices. The first data set comprises sales prices, which were provided by a large German leasing company. The second data set was obtained from AutoScout24, which is one of Germany's largest Internet platforms of used cars. In the remainder of this section, descriptions of these different data sets are presented and their strengths and weaknesses are discussed.

The leasing company's data set consists of various quarterly reports of more than 16,000 off-leases from October 2008 to December 2010. Information about the driven kilometers and age of each vehicle, which are calculated as the difference between the sales date and the first registration date of each lease contract, are obtained. To test the hypotheses, the data is restricted to vehicles that are older than 14 months because, as explained in Section 5.3, the sales of young automobiles may be subsidized by the scrappage premium. This may bias the results because a higher demand for employees' cars during the scrappage period may have generated higher prices for these relatively new vehicles. However, cars that are newer than 14 months only represent a small fraction of the entire data set with only 1,550 observations; thus, disregarding these automobiles should not affect the results. After these vehicles are omitted, this data set consists of 16,303 observations. Detailed information about motor characteristics such as the engine power, which is measured in kilowatts, and fuel type, such as petrol or diesel are available.

---

[118]Information about the sales volume is provided by Deutsche Automobil Treuhand (http://www.dat.de/en/home.html; last accessed: December 31, 2018) and data about new-car registrations and used-car transactions are provided by the Federal Motor Transport Authority (http://www.kba.de/EN/Home/home_node.html; last accessed: December 31, 2018).

Other car-specific attributes indicate whether a car has all-wheel drive and an automatic or manual gearbox and whether it is a station wagon or a sedan. The data also indicate the color, marque and model of each car. The sales results for each off-lease car is observed, which are corrected for damages, such as dents or damages to the paintwork. The pricing of the cars occurs by an online auction platform, in which only car dealers can bid for the off-leases.[119] Inflation-adjusted prices are utilized in this analysis; therefore, the sales results have to be adjusted by the consumer price index, which is provided by the Federal Agency of Statistics.[120] To establish homogenous groups of the provided sales results, the car classifications of the European Commission is employed to categorize the car models into the corresponding market segments.[121] An overview about the car classifications of the European Commission is presented in Table 2.1.

Summary statistics about all car-specific variables of the first data set are presented in Panel A of Table 5.1 and on the left-hand side of Table 5.2.

Table 5.1: **Summary Statistics - Continuous Variables**
The age is measured in years, mileage in thousand kilometers, power in kilowatt, the sales/offering price in euros.

Panel A: Data Set I

Variable	Mean	Sd	Min	p25	p50	p75	Max
Age	2.68	1.03	1.17	2.08	2.36	3.27	7.40
Mileage	69.87	46.77	0.00	32.51	59.60	92.10	359.03
Power	90.61	28.20	37.00	75.00	85.00	103.00	331.00
Sales price	11,715.95	4,596.88	3,031.80	9,328.00	11,261.65	13,164.00	55,359.50

Panel B: Data Set II

Variable	Mean	Sd	Min	p25	p50	p75	Max
Age	5.73	3.82	1.17	2.97	4.45	7.88	20.00
Mileage	85.58	55.74	0.00	40.60	76.96	120.43	316.30
Power	96.80	43.32	31.00	71.00	88.00	110.00	420.00
Offering price	12,849.90	10,812.95	422.00	6,399.00	10,700.00	16,480.00	204,900.00

---

[119]The auction prices are not identical to the prices for the final customer due to profit margins and guarantees by the car dealers. However, this study focuses on the *'price change'* due to the scrappage premium. Because of the high competitiveness in this market, it is expected that price effects caused by the introduction of the scrappage premium should also be observable when analyzing the prices paid by dealerships. The auction prices reveal the price reactions of well-informed market participants to market changes.

[120]The consumer price index is located at `https://www.destatis.de/EN/Homepage.html`; last accessed: December 31, 2018.

[121]Refer to European Commission (2002).

Table 5.2: **Summary Statistics - Categorical Variables**
　　　Car-specific dummy variables for 16,303 off-leases (left) and for 3,629,098 on-
　　　line advertisements (right). Car classification P is not clarified by the Com-
　　　mission of the European Communities. This characteristic is added to match
　　　pick-up trucks.

	Data Set I		Data Set II	
	Obs.	%	Obs.	%
Fuel				
Petrol	2,966	18.19	2,110,998	58.17
Diesel	13,337	81.81	1,518,100	41.83
All-wheel drive				
No	15,281	93.73	n.a.	n.a.
Yes	1,022	6.27		
Automatic				
No	10,307	63.22	n.a.	n.a.
Yes	5,996	36.78	n.a.	n.a.
Supplier				
Dealer	n.a.	n.a.	3,077,091	84.79
Private	n.a.	n.a.	552,007	15.21
Station wagon				
No	6,758	41.45	n.a.	n.a.
Yes	9,545	58.55	n.a.	n.a.
Marque				
Audi	1,969	12.08	301,318	8.30
BMW	0	0.00	361,958	9.97
Ford	0	0.00	263,374	7.26
Mercedes-Benz	0	0.00	369,581	10.18
Opel	0	0.00	384,838	10.60
Renault	0	0.00	208,639	5.75
Volkswagen	11,937	73.22	603,490	16.63
Volkswagen Comm. Vehicles	2,261	13.87	0	0.00
Others	136	0.83	1,135,900	31.31
Car Classification				
A	836	5.13	144,256	3.97
B	477	2.93	491,210	13.54
C	2,597	15.93	859,913	23,69
D	6,906	42.36	842,317	23.21
E	650	3.99	297,151	8.19
F	78	0.48	59,485	1.64
J	254	1.56	179,475	4.95
M	4,413	27.07	597,199	16.46
P	0	0.00	8,294	0.23
S	92	0.56	149,798	4.13

Table 5.3 lists the average price by vehicle segment and shows that price of small cars are less expensive than prices of large cars.

Table 5.3: **Average price by vehicle segment**
This table lists the average price by vehicle segment for data set I and data set II.

	Data set I	Data set II
A	5,726.87	5,598.61
B	6,313.05	7,154.60
C	9,878.47	9,899.74
D	11,841.11	12,957.34
E	16,172.66	17,231.16
F	22,163.15	31,395.8
J	29,098.83	22,548.43
M	11,941.66	12,104.22
P	n.a.	16,155.20
S	19,718.01	29,954.00

This leasing company's data set consists of different marques and models, which belong to the Volkswagen Group. It can be expected that the data set is representative of the German automobile market for the following reasons: First, the Volkswagen Group's overall market share of the total German automobile market is large (approximately 38% of all German new-car registrations in 2016[122]). Second, the Volkswagen Group has a large market share in each of the different car classifications. Third, the three subsidized models that have been subject to the greatest demand during the scrappage period belong to the Volkswagen Group, namely the Volkswagen Golf, Volkswagen Polo, and Skoda Fabia, which are represented in the data set of AutoScout24 (Federal Office of Economics and Export Control (2010)). Similarly, the registration numbers of new cars in 2014 confirm that the most favored models in each segment, with the exception of luxury cars and sport coupes, belong to the Volkswagen Group. Therefore, the results from this data set will most likely be valid for the entire German automobile market.

The second data set was provided by AutoScout24, which is an Internet platform of used cars. It contains offering prices of 6,294,824 advertisements, which were placed

---

[122]See Kraftfahrt-Bundesamt (2016).

during the years 2009 and 2010. These sale offers are reported on a quarterly basis and comprise the advertising price, driven kilometers, age, engine power, fuel type, marque and model of each car, as well as whether the salesperson is a professional dealer or a private household. This data set is truncated by excluding 1% of the cars with the highest mileage and 1% of the cars with the highest kilowatts and lowest kilowatts, respectively, and the same truncation is performed for the variable price for each car classification. The data is truncated because several observations contain implausible values and additionally it can be considered that the observations consist of offering prices. If the price of a used car is too high, it will not be sold, whereas very low prices may be attributed to damage to the car, which is not possible to control. This data set is restricted to cars that are older than 14 months and cars that are older than 20 years are eliminated because some advertisements of classic cars may distort the results; automotive enthusiasts that were selling these old cars listed high prices, which are difficult to capture. However, the price development of classic cars is not the focus of this thesis. The data set is restricted to cars with gasoline or diesel engines. Offers of trucks (over 3.5 t) and motorbikes are deleted to ensure that the data set only include passenger cars. Advertisements with missing records of some variables and automobiles, which are not classifiable as a certain car classification, were omitted. After omitting these vehicles, the data set consists of 3,629,098 observations. The main reason for this decline in the number of observations is that approximately 2.3 million vehicles are newer than 14 months. Descriptive statistics about the different variables of the revised second data set are presented in Panel B of Table 5.1 and on the right-hand side of Table 5.2 .

This second data set has several relevant advantages. First, due to the large number of observations the German used-car market is more adequately represented. Second, car models that do not belong to the Volkswagen Group are observed, too. Both aspects may be useful for verifying the results of the first data set and controlling the influences of the brand Volkswagen or specific well- or bad-performing car models of the Volkswagen Group. Thus, this second data set may improve the results regarding hypothesis H1. Third, the main advantage of the second data set is the presence of automobiles that are older than nine years, which may be scrapped during the scrappage scheme to attain the

€2,500 premium. Because lease contracts have a shorter duration than nine years, this approach does not apply to the first data set. This notion enables to analyze the shortage effect of scrapping nearly two million clunkers, which is considered in hypothesis H2.

There exist also some disadvantages of the second data set, which did not apply to the first data set. First, used-car prices prior to the introduction of the scrappage program cannot be observed because the observation period begins in January 2009, which is only two weeks before the scrappage scheme was introduced. Though, due to an increase in the budget from 1.5 billion to 5 billion at the end of the first quarter of 2009 and a lagged price adjustment, a significant price effect prior to the second quarter is not expected. This finding is confirmed by an increase in the number of submitted applications from 400 thousand to 1.2 million in the 14th calendar week after the introduction of an online application procedure to attain the scrappage premium on March 30, 2009.[123] Without knowledge of how successfully the scrappage scheme will be accepted by potential buyers of new cars, car dealers need some time to realize the reduced demand for small young cars until they adjust their pricing of these cars. Although some effects may also occur in the first quarter, it is expected that they were not substantial and that the main price shocks will be measurable in the subsequent quarters. To verify this expectation, the first data set is subsequently employed to demonstrate that no statistically significant price effect is measurable in the first quarter of 2009; rather, the main price effects can be subsequently observed. This finding verifies the applicability of the second data set, which covers the first quarter of 2009 prior to an increase in the budget, as the comparison period.

Second, the data of the Internet platform does not include transaction prices, which are contained in the off-leases data set, but advertising prices. This may cause a higher variation in the prices in the second data set because private persons may not always behave rationally and may not be as acquainted with the valuation of used cars as dealers. However, they can follow already existing price offerings, which are dominated by professional car dealers, as indicated by Table 5.2, which account for approximately 85%

---

[123]Refer to Federal Office of Economics and Export Control (2010).

of all advertisements. Hence, even if it cannot be ruled out that some offerings are not serious attempts to sell a car, this is highly unlikely for the major share of the observations because dealers do not use their cars for their own purpose and are interested in a swift resale. Furthermore, it is not expected that the extent of price negotiations are affected by the scrappage premium. As shown by Morton et al. (2011), price negotiations are mainly influenced by the final customers' knowledge about the reservation price and the obtaining of settlement offers;[124] it seems implausible that this should be affected by the policy. Moreover, the 'price change' of different car segments due to the scrappage premium is subsequently analyzed. It is assumed that the prices of the first data set are slightly lower than the prices in the second data set because they do not contain any profit margins of the dealers. However, there is no reason to believe that the potential difference between the advertising and the transaction prices is systematically different before and after the introduction of the scrappage premium. For these reasons, problems by using advertising prices are not expected;[125] Instead, advertising prices enable to verify hypotheses H3a, H3b and H3c.

Third, this data set contains less information about specific car characteristics, such as automatic or color, than the first data set. However, the majority of the explanatory power is attributable to the variables age and mileage, which explain nearly 60% of the variation in the prices (with power, even over 80%).

5.5.2 Empirical Strategy

Subsequently, the hypotheses from Section 5.4.2 are tested, which refer to the impact of the German scrappage scheme on prices in the second-hand car market, using OLS regression methods with robust standard errors. For the dependent variable *sales value* logarithmized values are utilized. To analyze different effects of the scrappage bonus on different car sizes, as described in Section 5.4.2, difference-in-differences estimators are

---

[124] Customers can easily observe comparable used-car prices by using the search functions of Internet used-car platforms. See also Kwon et al. (2015) for impacts on the bargaining power.

[125] Hanemann (1991) and Shogren et al. (1994) showed that in a competitive market with close substitutes the willingness to pay and the willingness to accept do not diverge.

employed. For this purpose, two different treatment groups are constructed. Treatment group 1 contains small young cars and enables to measure the demand effect. The variable *small* is one if a car belongs to segment A or B and zero otherwise. The variable *young* is also a dummy variable, which identifies cars younger than four years. [126] In the analyses with treatment group 1, the reference group is defined as cars older than four years from the other segments if they are not defined as a clunker (see the following definition of clunker/treatment group 2). It is expected that these segments should only be slightly affected by the scrappage scheme due to their high average prices, as discussed in Section 5.4.2. This notion is undergirded by new-car registrations in Figure 5.2 because the number of registrations of cars from larger car segments, with the exception of segment C, were nearly on the same level during the scrapping scheme than prior to the scheme. Despite the large number of new-car registrations during the scrappage scheme of segment C, segment C is not employed as part of the treatment group because mean primary market prices are also very high for this segment. That is why a greater effect is expected using the segments of smaller cars A and B as the treatment group 1.

Even if it is not possible on the basis of the covered time period of the data set to analyze common trends prior to the introduction of the scrappage scheme empirically, a corresponding result of Nau (2012) can be used. According to Nau (2012), used-car prices are not affected by macro-economic developments but rather by the developments in the primary and secondary market, which can lead to a shift in demand for used cars. In her study, Nau (2012) empirically analyzes the price developments of different three years old car models of the major segments. For this reason, her results regarding cars of the small and large segments are representative for the treatment group and reference group of this study, respectively. The analysis covers the time period prior to the introduction of the scrappage scheme and also focuses on the German used-car market. As the investigated cars are amongst the cars with the highest registration numbers in their segment, the results of Nau (2012) show that the reference group and the treatment group have parallel trends prior to the introduction of the scrappage premium.

---

[126]Alternative definitions of young cars are also used, which did not substantially affect the results.

To measure the shortage effect caused by the scrappage of nearly two million old cars, a treatment group 2 is constructed, which consists of clunkers that can be identified as follows: A dummy variable *clunker* is introduced, which is one if the age of the car exceeds the required age for which the average car value of the respective car classification is less than €2,500. Particularly, it is considered that not all cars, which exceed the necessary age of nine years to be applicable for receiving the scrappage premium, did attain a value less than €2,500. Rational car holders would not scrap their cars if their values exceeded the scrappage premium. Table 5.4 provides an overview for each segment regarding the age criteria to be defined as a clunker.

Table 5.4: **Definition of Clunker**
This table lists the age of a used car for each car classification, after which the average value is less than the scrappage bonus of €2,500.

Car Classification	Age
A	11 years
B	11 years
C	13 years
D	16 years
E	-
F	-
J	-
M	-
P	-
S	-

The average values of cars of segments A, B, C, and D decrease below €2,500; this case only applies if the cars are at least eleven years old. Cars of higher categories are more expensive than the scrappage premium even if they are very old. This finding coincides with the final report of the Federal Office of Economics and Export Control, which indicates that approximately 75% of the scrapped vehicles belong to low car classifications Federal Office of Economics and Export Control (2010).

The reference group for the analyses that use treatment group 2 consists of all cars older than 4 years that are not defined as a clunker. Incorporating the reference group in the analysis enables to control for possible price effects of the market crisis, which both treatment and reference group were exposed. Nevertheless, the reference groups may also be affected by the scrappage scheme because all cars are substitutes among each other and therefore the scrappage premium may have modified the relative value of all cars to some extent. However, because of the heterogeneity of cars of different vintages and segments, greater price effects for the treatment groups than for cars of the reference groups are expected. To take this concerns into account, additional robustness checks are provided in Section 5.7, verifying the validity of the obtained results.

The period in which car-holders can utilize the scrappage bonus is modeled by dummy variables, which equal one if the used cars were sold during the accelerated vehicle retirement program and equal zero otherwise. *scrappage1* =1 is defined for the first quarter of 2009, which is the period of the scrappage program before the budget was increased, and *scrappage2* =1 for the second and third quarter of 2009 (short-run effect), which entails the period of the scrappage program after the enhancement of the budget to 5 billion euros, or *scrappage2* =1 if the car was sold between Q2/2009 and Q4/2010 (mid-run effect). The dummy variable *private_ sale* indicates whether the online advertisement was placed by a private household (*private_ sale*=1) or a professional car dealer.

To determine the different price development between the treatment and the reference group, all regression coefficients of interest, which belong to an interaction with the scrappage dummy, are summed. The following equation is employed:

$$DiD = (Treatment_{t+1} - Treatment_t) - (Reference_{t+1} - Reference_t) \qquad (5.6)$$

Generally, the difference-in-differences estimator (DiD) is defined as the difference between the effect on the treatment group in period t and t+1 and the effect on the reference group in period t and $t + 1$, ceteris paribus, which is expressed by Equation 5.6.[127] In the subsequent analyses of hypotheses H1 - H3, several control variables are considered, such as *age*, *mileage* and *power*. These variables are derived from existing studies,

---

[127]See also Appendix 5.9.1 for further information regarding the difference-in-differences estimation method.

which employ hedonic regression methods to explain the market value of used cars.[128] The explanatory variables of *age*, *mileage* and *power* are modeled by linear and quadratic expressions to incorporate higher deterioration for the initial years and kilometers and a higher value impact of each kilowatt for less powerful cars.[129] The dummy variables *automatic*, *all-wheel drive*, *diesel*, *sedan*, *private_ sale*, *color* and *brand* are considered as additional control variables. Overall, the findings for these variables coincide with the results in the literature and are therefore not explicitly reported, but summarized as *car-specific controls* to indicate that all available car information are considerd.[130]

5.6 Empirical Results

5.6.1 Price Effect for Small Young Cars

In this section, it is analyzed whether prices of small young vehicles are affected by the subsidy during the scrappage scheme. According to hypotheses H1a and H1b, it is expected that the prices of small young cars decline as a consequence of the scrappage scheme; this effect occurs in the short-run and the medium-run. To analyze this effect, it is considered that the isolated price development of these cars may be influenced by the behavior of the total market of used cars. Against this background, a difference-in-differences estimator is implemented and it is tested whether the price development of small young cars (treatment group 1) behave differently than the price development of cars older than four years of the larger car segments that are not a clunker (reference group), for which it is assumed that they are only slightly affected by the scrappage program. Interaction terms

---

[128] Hedonic regression approaches that focus on car-specific features and their valuation over time are detailed in Ohta and Griliches (1976), Gordon (1990) and Dexheimer (2003). A detailed overview about the determinants of residual values is provided by Nau (2012).

[129] In alternative model specifications, the linear terms and a logarithmic transformation of age, mileage and power are implemented. It is discovered that this approach does not substantially change the results; thus, the transformation with the highest explanatory power is employed. This finding is consistent with the findings of Wykoff (1970), Ackerman (1973) and Ohta and Griliches (1976), who identify non-linear depreciation rates.

[130] Wykoff (1970), Ackerman (1973) and Ohta and Griliches (1976) show that cars do not depreciate at a constant rate but show different patterns during different time periods and for different models; they propose exponential decreasing rates.

between all combinations of the variables *small, young*, and *scrappage1* or *scrappage2* are constructed to determine the difference-in-differences estimator. In the first step, the results are presented using the first data set of the leasing company, for which the quarter prior to the introduction of the scrappage scheme can be observed. The regression results are presented in Table 5.5.

Table 5.5: **Data Set I: Price Effects for Small Young Cars**
This table lists the results of OLS regressions with robust standard errors for the data set of the leasing company. Regression (A.1) shows the results for the differences between the quarter prior to the introduction of the scrappage scheme (Q4/2008, pre-scrappage) and Q1/2009 (scrappage1), regressions (A.2) and (A.3) show the results for the period after the increase in the budget of the subsidy (scrappage2) and regressions (A.4) and (A.5) indicate the different effect between the two scrappage periods. The last four regression are divided into a short-run effect (scrappage2=1 if the sales date fell in Q2 or Q3/2009) and a medium-run effect (scrappage2=1 if the sales date fell between Q2/2009 and Q4/2010) of the scrappage scheme. The robust standard errors are reported in parentheses. The symbols †,*,** and ***, indicate statistical significance at the 10% level, 5% level, 1% level and 0.1% level, respectively.

	(A.1)	(A.2)	(A.3)	(A.4)	(A.5)
	Pre-scrappage vs. Scrappage1	Pre-scrappage vs. Scrappage2		Scrappage1 vs. Scrappage2	
		Short-run	Medium-run	Short-run	Medium-run
Scrappage1	-0.044***				
	(0.013)				
Scrappage1 × Young	0.033*				
	(0.014)				
Scrappage1 × Small	0.207				
	(0.164)				
Scrappage1 × Young × Small	-0.281†				
	(0.167)				
Scrappage2		-0.091***	-0.007	-0.049***	0.043***
		(0.013)	(0.012)	(0.012)	(0.011)
Scrappage2 × Young		0.031*	-0.070***	0.008	-0.115***
		(0.014)	(0.013)	(0.013)	(0.012)
Scrappage2 × Small		0.207	0.159	0.023	-0.052
		(0.134)	(0.151)	(0.047)	(0.045)
Scrappage2 × Young × Small		-0.286*	-0.185	-0.035	0.097*
		(0.137)	(0.153)	(0.049)	(0.047)
Young	-0.049**	-0.063***	0.027†	-0.046**	0.067***
	(0.019)	(0.015)	(0.015)	(0.015)	(0.014)
Small	-0.22	-0.169	-0.274†	0.008	-0.063
	(0.161)	(0.134)	(0.151)	(0.047)	(0.044)
Young × Small	0.038	0.011	0.062	-0.234***	-0.219***
	(0.163)	(0.137)	(0.153)	(0.048)	(0.046)
Constant	8.743***	8.776***	8.834***	8.750***	8.787***
	(0.063)	(0.050)	(0.024)	(0.043)	(0.022)
Car-specific controls	Yes	Yes	Yes	Yes	Yes
Observations	2,619	5,328	14,809	5,697	15,178
R²	0.899	0.899	0.841	0.902	0.843
Adjusted R²	0.898	0.899	0.840	0.902	0.843

The first regression (A.1) was implemented for the quarters Q4/2008 and Q1/2009 to analyze significant effects in the first quarter of the accelerated vehicle retirement program prior to an increase in the budget (*scrappage1*), as described in Section 5.5.2. Regressions (A.2) and (A.3) analyze the differences between the period prior to the scrappage program (Q4/2008) and the period of the scrappage program after the increase in the budget. The short-run effect is considered by defining *scrappage2*=1 if the car was sold in Q2 and Q3/2009[131] and the medium-run effect is considered by defining *scrappage2*=1 if the car was sold between Q2/2009 and Q4/2010. The price effect during the scrappage scheme and the effect of potential pull-forward effects in the period after the subsidy can be measured. The observations are restricted to Q4/2008 and the period for which scrappage2 is equal to one. Regressions (A.4) and (A.5) examine the different price developments between *scrappage1* and *scrappage2* by including only the observations for which *scrappage1* or *scrappage2* are equal to one.

Using the example of regression (A.1), the coefficients of the combinations of the dummy variables of small young cars are inserted as the treatment group and large cars older than four years that are not defined as a clunker as the reference group in Equation 5.6. The control variables do not have to be included because they are held equal in both periods. The periods are defined as the quarter prior to the introduction of the scrappage scheme and the subsequent quarter. Thus, inserting the coefficients of regression (A.1) in Equation 5.6 results in the following equation:

$$
\begin{aligned}
DiD_{small} =\ & (young + small + young \times small + scrappage1 + scrappage1 \times young \\
& + scrappage1 \times small + scrappage1 \times young \times small \\
& - (young + small + young \times small)) - scrappage1 \\
=\ & scrappage1 \times young + scrappage1 \times small \\
& + scrappage1 \times young \times small \\
=\ & 0.033 + 0.207 - 0.281 = -0.041
\end{aligned} \tag{5.7}
$$

---

[131] The third quarter of 2009 is employed as the end of the scrappage program because the budget was exhausted at the end of September.

With this approach, the difference-in-differences estimators of regressions (A.2)-(A.5) can be easily computed by substituting *scrappage2* for *scrappage1* in this expression. Using the Wald test, it is examined whether the estimators are significantly different from zero. Table 5.6 lists the difference-in-differences estimators, which are based on the coefficients listed in Table 5.5, and the results of the Wald test.

Table 5.6: **Data Set I: Effect of Scrappage for Small Young Cars (DiD)**
This table lists the difference-in-differences estimators for regressions (A.1)-(A.5) from Table 5.5 using small young cars as the treatment group and old and large cars that are not defined as a clunker as the reference group. Using the Wald test, the symbols $^\dagger, ^*, ^{**}$ and ***, indicate statistical significance at the 10% level, 5% level, 1% level and 0.1% level, respectively.

	(A.1)	(A.2)	(A.3)	(A.4)	(A.5)
	Pre-scrappage vs. Scrappage1	Pre-scrappage vs. Scrappage2		Scrappage1 vs. Scrappage2	
		Short-run	Medium-run	Short-run	Medium-run
Diff-in-diff estimator	-4.06%	-4.87%†	-9.67%***	-0.48%	-6.97%***

It can be discovered that the difference-in-differences estimator is negative for all regressions, which indicates that small young cars exhibit a greater decrease during the scrappage program and after the increase of the budget than the cars of the reference group. Some coefficients are not significant. The effect in regression (A.1) reveals that a significant influence of the subsidy cannot be detected in the first quarter of 2009; however, the coefficient of -4.06 percentage points indicates that the economic effect could be relevant even if it is not statistically significant. This finding is consistent with the assumption in Section 5.5.2.

The negative effect becomes significant by considering the difference between the period prior to the subsidy and after the increase in the budget (regressions (A.2) and (A.3)). In the short-run, this effect is slightly significant at the ten percent level; in the medium-run, however, it is highly significant, both statistically and economically. These results indicate that the prices of small young cars decrease approximately -4.87 percentage points more than cars that were not affected by the subsidy during the period of the scrappage scheme (after an increase in the budget). This effect is even substantially higher when the year after the subsidy is included and -9.67 percentage points are attained. Thus, the medium-run effect is even higher than the short-run effect, which indicates pull-forward effects of car sales. These results confirm the hypotheses H1a and H1b.

The obtained results are verified with the second data set of the secondary market, which is substantially larger and more representative for the German car market. For this data set, the first quarter of 2009, which is the quarter prior the increase in the budget of the subsidy, is declared as the reference period. This declaration is feasible because any significant difference between the period Q4/2008 and Q1/2009 could not be identified in regression (A.1). Of course, this could be the reason of the small number of observations of data set I. The coefficient of -4.06 percentage points is relatively low and may indicate a negative price effect in the first quarter of the scrappage program, but because of the missing significance this is only a random result and the effect cannot be distinguished from zero. Nevertheless, evidence for an additional price effect after the increase in the budget is found. Although the difference between the treatment group *scrappage1* and the reference group *scrappage2* was not significant in the short-run (see regression (A.4)), a highly significant result in the medium-run (regression (A.5)) is observed. The difference-in-differences estimator in regression (A.4) has the assumed sign; thus, this coefficient may become significant if the data set consists of more observations. As a consequence, the effect of the scrappage scheme may be less distinct in the short-run when using the second data set. It can be expected that the second data set is appropriate for testing the price effects of the scrappage scheme, particularly because even smaller economic effects can be detected with these data due to the large sample size. The regression results of the second data set, which contains sales advertisements from the Internet platform, are shown in Table 5.7.

Regression (B.1) and (B.2) show the results for the differences between the period of the subsidy prior to the increase in the budget (Q1/2009) and the period after the increase for the complete data set. Because it is possible to observe whether the sales advertisement was placed by a car dealer or a household, the sample is split into offerings of dealers ((B.3) and (B.4)) and private offers for sale ((B.5) and (B.6)). The regressions are divided into a short-run time horizon and a medium-run time horizon. The difference-in-

Table 5.7: **Data Set II: Effect of Scrappage for Small Young Cars**
This table lists the results of OLS regressions with robust standard errors for the data set of the Internet platform of used cars. Small young cars are employed as the treatment group and old and large cars as the reference group. Regressions (B.1) and (B.2) show the results for the differences between the period of the subsidy prior to the increase in the budget (Q1/2009) and the period after the increase (scrappage2) for the complete sample, regressions (B.3) and (B.4) show the results only for the dealers' sales offerings and (B.5) and (B.6) only show the results for private advertisements. The regressions are divided into a short-run effect (scrappage2=1 if the sales date fell in Q2 or Q3/2009) and a medium-run effect (scrappage2=1 if the sales date fell between Q2/2009 and Q4/2010). The robust standard errors are reported in parentheses. The symbols †,*,** and ***, indicate statistical significance at the 10% level, 5% level, 1% level and 0.1% level, respectively.

	(B.1)	(B.2)	(B.3)	(B.4)	(B.5)	(B.6)
	Full sample		Dealer		Private	
	Short-run	Medium-run	Short-run	Medium-run	Short-run	Medium-run
Scrappage2	-0.009***	-0.010***	-0.011***	-0.012***	-0.003	-0.004**
	(0.001)	(0.001)	(0.001)	(0.001)	(0.002)	(0.002)
Scrappage2 × Small	0.016***	0.008***	0.018***	0.010***	0.004	-0.000
	(0.002)	(0.002)	(0.002)	(0.002)	(0.004)	(0.004)
Scrappage2 × Young	-0.006***	0.004***	-0.004***	0.005***	-0.013***	0.006*
	(0.001)	(0.001)	(0.001)	(0.001)	(0.004)	(0.003)
Scrappage2 × Small × Young	-0.018***	-0.019***	-0.020***	-0.021***	-0.006	-0.011
	(0.002)	(0.002)	(0.003)	(0.002)	(0.008)	(0.007)
Small	-0.104***	-0.095***	-0.103***	-0.094***	-0.098***	-0.095***
	(0.002)	(0.002)	(0.002)	(0.002)	(0.004)	(0.004)
Young	-0.042***	-0.057***	-0.031***	-0.046***	-0.123***	-0.133***
	(0.001)	(0.001)	(0.001)	(0.001)	(0.004)	(0.003)
Small × Young	-0.018***	-0.014***	-0.022**	-0.020***	-0.012†	-0.004
	(0.002)	(0.002)	(0.002)	(0.002)	(0.007)	(0.007)
Private_Sale	-0.070***	-0.068***				
	(0.001)	(0.001)				
Constant	9.145***	9.153***	9.047***	9.061***	9.226***	9.217***
	(0.003)	(0.002)	(0.003)	(0.002)	(0.010)	(0.006)
Car-specific controls	Yes	Yes	Yes	Yes	Yes	Yes
Observations	1,530,471	3,469,112	1,343,679	2,992,977	186,792	476,135
R^2	0.873	0.878	0.873	0.878	0.832	0.837
Adjusted R^2	0.873	0.878	0.873	0.878	0.832	0.837

differences estimator of each regression is computed using Equation 5.6 and the procedure of Equation 5.7. The results are listed in Table 5.8 and tested for significance using the Wald test.

Table 5.8: **Data Set II: Effect of Scrappage for Small Young Cars (DiD)**
This table lists the difference-in-differences estimators using small young cars as the treatment and old and large cars that are not defined as a clunkers as the reference group. Using the Wald test, the symbols *,** and ***, indicate statistical significance at the 5% level, 1% level and 0.1% level, respectively.

	(B.1)	(B.2)	(B.3)	(B.4)	(B.5)	(B.6)
	Full sample		Dealer		Private	
	Short-run	Medium-run	Short-run	Medium-run	Short-run	Medium-run
Diff-in-diff estimator	-0.74%***	-0.69%***	-0.54%***	-0.60%***	-1.43%*	-0.47%

The results of the second data set confirm the effects, which are observed using the data of the leasing company. The sign of every difference-in-differences estimator is negative and significant, with the exception of the medium-run effect of private advertisements (regression (B.6)). It is not possible to detect the same magnitude of the effect of the different price development between the treatment group and the reference group as it is observed by using the first data set. The prices of small young cars decrease by approximately one percentage point more than the prices of older cars of the remaining segments.[132] It can be discovered that prices of small young cars, which were preferentially bought during the subsidy, exhibit a greater decrease than the prices of cars of the reference group; this price effect continued and even increased after the budget of the subsidy was exhausted. With respect to welfare aspects, the demand shock for small young cars causes a downward shift of the demand curve for these cars and a welfare loss in the secondary market.

---

[132]The reduced economic significance compared to the results of the first data set is likely a consequence of the selected reference period Q1/2009, which is attributed to limited data availability.

5.6.2 Shortage of Old Clunkers

Next, it is analyzed whether the shortage of old clunkers, which were feasible for the replacement during the scrappage scheme, caused an increase in used-car prices for vehicles of this group. Because the first data set only contains off-leases newer than eight years, the price effect of a shortage of old clunkers cannot be measured for these cars with the data set of the leasing company. For this reason, this section focuses on the second data set, which also contains observations for very old cars.

An interaction between *scrappage2* and *clunker* is employed and regression analyses are performed to obtain the difference-in-differences estimator for clunkers during the scrappage program, which equals

$$DiD_{clunker} = scrappage2 \times clunker. \tag{5.8}$$

In Table 5.9, the regression results are presented. The first two regressions use the entire data set and are divided into a short-run effect (C.1) and a medium-run effect (C.2). The same regressions are performed for car offerings by dealers ((C.3) and (C.4)) and private advertisements ((C.5) and (C.6)). Next, the difference-in-differences estimators are derived from the regression results. The results are presented in Table 5.10.

The results confirm the supply hypotheses: the prices for old clunkers increased during the scrappage scheme (H2a) and in the medium-run (H2b). Positive effects that range from 2.13 to 5.73 percentage points are observed, which are highly statistically and economically significant. A much stronger effect on prices of car dealers is revealed in the medium-run compared with the short-run, which is diametrical for private offerings for sale. For private advertisements, also a positive effect is observed in the short-run, which is slightly stronger than the effect for dealers; however, this effect decreases in the medium-run, which contradicts the observed effect on car dealers' prices. Therefore, the question arises of whether a short-term price effect for clunkers of private sales advertisements is observable, which ended after the budget of the scrappage scheme was exhausted. For

Table 5.9: **Data Set II: Effect of Scrappage for Clunkers**
This table lists the results of OLS regressions with robust standard errors for the data set of the Internet platform of used cars. Clunkers as defined in Table 5.4 are used as the treatment group and the other cars as the reference group. Regressions (C.1) and (C.2) show the results for the differences between the period of the subsidy prior to the increase in the budget (Q1/2009) and the period after the increase (scrappage2) for the complete sample, regressions (C.3) and (C.4) show the results for dealers' sales offerings and (C.5) and (C.6) show the results for private advertisements. The regressions are divided into a short-run effect (scrappage2=1 if the sales date fell in Q2 or Q3/2009) and a medium-run effect (scrappage2=1 if the sales date fell between Q2/2009 and Q4/2010). The robust standard errors are reported in parentheses. The symbols †,*,** and ***, indicate statistical significance at the 10% level, 5% level, 1% level and 0.1% level, respectively.

	(C.1)	(C.2)	(C.3)	(C.4)	(C.5)	(C.6)
	Full sample		Dealer		Private	
	Short-run	Medium-run	Short-run	Medium-run	Short-run	Medium-run
Scrappage2	-0.007***	-0.008***	-0.009***	-0.010***	-0.004*	-0.006***
	(0.001)	(0.001)	(0.001)	(0.001)	(0.002)	(0.002)
Clunker	-0.325***	-0.312***	-0.345***	-0.343***	-0.264***	-0.241***
	(0.004)	(0.004)	(0.005)	(0.005)	(0.006)	(0.005)
Scrappage2 × Clunker	0.034***	0.042***	0.030***	0.057***	0.034***	0.021***
	(0.004)	(0.004)	(0.006)	(0.005)	(0.006)	(0.005)
Private_Sale	-0.067***	-0.071***				
	(0.001)	(0.001)				
Constant	9.230***	9.219***	9.133***	9.125***	9.167***	9.153***
	(0.004)	(0.003)	(0.004)	(0.003)	(0.010)	(0.006)
Car-specific controls	Yes	Yes	Yes	Yes	Yes	Yes
Observations	867,517	2,051,598	686,888	1,580,513	180,629	471,085
R^2	0.849	0.855	0.848	0.854	0.823	0.832
Adjusted R^2	0.849	0.855	0.848	0.854	0.823	0.832

Table 5.10: **Data Set II: Effect of Scrappage for Clunkers (DiD)**
This table lists the difference-in-differences estimators using clunkers as defined in Table 5.4 as the treatment and the other cars older than four years as the reference group. The symbols *,** and ***, indicate statistical significance at the 5% level, 1% level and 0.1% level, respectively.

	(C.1)	(C.2)	(C.3)	(C.4)	(C.5)	(C.6)
	Full sample		Dealer		Private	
	Short-run	Medium-run	Short-run	Medium-run	Short-run	Medium-run
Diff-in-diff estimator	3.43%***	4.18%***	2.95%***	5.73%***	3.37%***	2.13%***

this reason, regression (C.6) is repeated by excluding the period of the scrappage scheme after the increase in the budget (Q2 and Q3/2009). The price effect after the end of the scrappage program reduces to 1.74 percentage points; however, it remains highly significant (p=0.001). This finding also supports hypothesis H3c because these results are consistent with the argument that private sales offerings include the option value for the possibility to scrap the old vehicle and receive the premium. A higher effect for private advertisements compared with dealer sales offerings confirms this conjecture. Evidence for hypothesis H3b is also found because the prices of car dealers increased after the end of the subsidy, which is plausible because car dealers may have more information about the development of secondary markets than households. However, they probably need some time to assess the shortage effect of nearly two million clunkers, which is why a higher effect can be observed in the medium-run.

The shortage of old clunkers caused by the scrappage program generates an increase in the prices of the remaining cars of this type and an upwards shift of the supply curve, which causes welfare losses in the secondary market. Because low-income households primarily demand old clunkers, it can be concluded that these households are disadvantaged by this political intervention.

In the next section, the different price effects between dealer offerings and private sales offerings are analyzed.

5.6.3 Price Effects between Dealers' and Private Sales

In this section, the differences in the pricing of used cars between car dealers and households are investigated as suggested by H3a, H3b and H3c. It is expected that the prices of privately advertised clunkers exhibited a greater increase than the prices of professional car dealers during the scrappage scheme due to the option value of receiving the scrappage premium. In the medium-run, stronger effects for car dealers are assumed due to their superior ability to assess market prices. For young cars, different price effects are not expected due to the transparency in the secondary market for these vehicles. All

interaction combinations between *small, young, scrappage2* and *private_sale* are added
to the regression equation to determine different pricing behaviors between dealer advertisements and private advertisements for small young cars and all interactions between
clunker, scrappage2 and *private_sale* to measure the different effects for clunkers. The
data set is not split into dealer offerings and private sales offerings as previously noted.
Table 5.11 lists the results of the corresponding regression analyses.

The difference-in-differences estimators, which explain the different price effects for
private sales between the relevant two periods (during the scrappage scheme and prior
to the scrappage scheme) compared with the price effects of dealers between these two
periods, are presented in Table 5.12. The Wald test is employed to test for statistical
significance.

Regressions (D.1) and (D.2) analyze the short- and medium-run effects between dealers'
and private advertisements for small young cars. In regressions (D.3) and (D.4), the same
analysis is performed for the different effects regarding old clunkers. The difference-in-
differences estimators for small young cars (regressions (D.1) and (D.2)) are expressed as
the following sum of the regression coefficients:

$$
\begin{aligned}
DiD_{small} = \; & private\_sale \times scrappage2 + private\_sale \times scrappage2 \times small \\
& + private\_sale \times scrappage2 \times young \\
& + private\_sale \times scrappage2 \times small \times young.
\end{aligned} \tag{5.9}
$$

For old clunkers they are expressed as the following sum of the regression coefficients:

$$
\begin{aligned}
DiD_{clunker} = \; & private\_sale \times scrappage2 \\
& + private\_sale \times scrappage2 \times clunker.
\end{aligned} \tag{5.10}
$$

These expressions are analogous to Equation 5.6.

The difference-in-differences estimator of regression (D.3) is significantly positive, which
indicates that even if the prices of old cars increased during the subsidy period for both

Table 5.11: **Data Set II: Effect of Scrappage - Private vs. Dealer**
This table lists the results of OLS regressions with robust standard errors for the data set of the Internet platform of used cars. The different price development between sales offerings of dealers during the scrappage scheme (scrappage2) and the previous period (Q1/2009) compared with price changes in private sales advertisements for the same periods are analyzed. Regressions (D.1) and (D.2) show the results for the price effect of small young cars for these different groups in the short-run (scrappage2=1 if the sales date fell in Q2 or Q3/2009) and the medium-run (scrappage2=1 if the sales date fell between Q2/2009 and Q4/2010); regressions (D.3) and (D.4) show similar results for the pricing of clunkers. The robust standard errors are reported in parentheses. The symbols †,*,** and ***, indicate statistical significance at the 10% level, 5% level, 1% level and 0.1% level, respectively.

	(D.1)	(D.2)	(D.3)	(D.4)
	Young & Small		Clunker	
	Short-run	Medium-run	Short-run	Medium-run
Private_Sale × Scrappage2	0.008***	0.005**	0.006**	0.002
	(0.002)	(0.002)	(0.002)	(0.002)
Private_Sale × Scrappage2 × Small	-0.011*	-0.007†		
	(0.005)	(0.004)		
Private_Sale × Scrappage2 × Young	-0.009*	0.003		
	(0.004)	(0.003)		
Private_Sale × Scrappage2 × Small × Young	0.010	0.006		
	(0.008)	(0.007)		
Private_Sale × Scrappage2 × Clunker			0.010	-0.032***
			(0.008)	(0.007)
Private_Sale	-0.076***	-0.074***	-0.075***	-0.074***
	(0.002)	(0.002)	(0.002)	(0.002)
Scrappage2	-0.011***	-0.011***	-0.008***	-0.009***
	(0.001)	(0.001)	(0.001)	(0.001)
Clunker			-0.340***	-0.328***
			(0.005)	(0.005)
Small	-0.097***	-0.088***		
	(0.002)	(0.002)		
Young	-0.044***	-0.059***		
	(0.001)	(0.001)		
Small × Young	-0.025***	-0.022***		
	(0.002)	(0.002)		
Private_Sale × Small	-0.039***	-0.039***		
	(0.004)	(0.004)		
Private_Sale × Young	0.032***	0.032***		
	(0.003)	(0.003)		
Private_Sale × Small × Young	0.026***	0.025***		
	(0.007)	(0.007)		
Private_Sale × Clunker			0.040***	0.038***
			(0.007)	(0.007)
Scrappage2 × Small	0.018***	0.009***		
	(0.002)	(0.002)		
Scrappage2 × Young	-0.005***	0.004*		
	(0.001)	(0.001)		
Scrappage2 × Clunker			0.028***	0.055***
			(0.006)	(0.005)
Scrappage2 × Small × Young	-0.019***	0.020***		
	(0.003)	(0.002)		
Constant	9.075***	9.085***	9.161***	9.147***
	(0.002)	(0.002)	(0.004)	(0.003)
Car-specific controls	Yes	Yes	Yes	Yes
Observations	1,530,471	3,469,112	867,517	2,051,598
R^2	0.873	0.878	0.849	0.855
Adjusted R^2	0.873	0.878	0.849	0.855

Table 5.12: **Data Set II: Effect of Scrappage - Private vs. Dealer (DiD)**

This table lists the difference-in-differences estimators using private sales offerings as the treatment and dealer offerings as the reference group. The symbols *,** and ***, indicate statistical significance at the 5% level, 1% level and 0.1% level, respectively.

	(D.1)	(D.2)	(D.3)	(D.4)
	Young & Small		Clunker	
	Short-run	Medium-run	Short-run	Medium-run
Diff-in-diff estimator	-0.18%	0.66%	1.57%†	-2.95%***

dealers' and private offerings, the effect of increasing prices was significantly higher for private offerings. A possible reason for this stronger effect is that households had the option of receiving €2,500 if they decided to scrap their old car and buy a new car during the scrappage scheme. Therefore, they want to be compensated for losing this option if they decide to sell their old vehicle in the secondary market, which generates a higher price increase for private sales offerings than for dealers' offerings. These findings confirm the hypothesis H3c.

In the medium-run (regression (D.4)), the opposite effect occurs. The average used-car prices of old clunkers, which were offered by car dealers, increased by approximately 2.95 percentage points greater than the average used-car prices of old cars that were advertised by households. This effect is highly statistically and economically significant and can be explained by better possibilities for car dealers to observe developments in the secondary market and to rapidly react to changes in demand and supply. Car dealers can profit from better sales channels and customer contacts. Therefore, they are able to provide an assessment of the used-car value that is more precise than the assessments obtained by households. In fact, the option value of private households, which leads to a higher price increase for old clunkers which were advertised by households during the scrappage scheme, even diminished the medium-run effect. As it was ascertained in Section 5.6.2, some positive price effects are still observable for private sales advertisements of old clunkers; however, these positive price effects are less pronounced than the positive price effects for dealer offerings. Thus, private market participants seem to be aware of the lower supply of old cars. These findings are consistent with hypothesis H3b.

The difference-in-differences estimators of regression (D.1) and (D.2) do not show any significant size. Therefore, the prices of small young cars of dealers' and private sales offerings changed in the same proportion after the introduction of the subsidy, which is in line with hypothesis H3a. The reason for the lack of different pricing behaviors may be due to the transparency of used-car prices of small young cars in the secondary market. Owners of young cars can observe reference prices of their cars because they will easily find a comparable matching by searching for the same car on an online platform of used cars, which is frequently not possible for old clunkers because there are substantially fewer advertisements for older cars. The likely reason is that the older is a car, the higher is the probability that it breaks down, e.g., due to engine damage or an accident, which causes it to leave the secondary market. In contrast to the market for young cars, the market for old cars is dominated by private advertisements.

To sum up, the results of Table 5.12 show a different price development between dealers' sales advertisements and private sales advertisements when prices at the secondary market are not easily observable (regression (D.3) and (D.4)). In the case of a transparent secondary market, the pricing of used cars uniformly occurs (regression (D.1) and (D.2)) because households can easily determine the price offerings of comparable advertisements. This finding indicates information asymmetries in the used-car market because car dealers charge more appropriate prices than households as a reaction to the shortage of old clunkers (regression (D.4)), which confirms othe hypotheses H3a, H3b and H3c.

5.7 Robustness Checks

5.7.1 Alternative Reference Group - Price Effects for Small Young Cars

One possible problem of using the difference-in-difference estimation method may be that the reference group is not completely unaffected by the scrappage scheme. Reason for this is that all cars are substitutes among each other and therefore the scrappage scheme must have modified the relative value of all cars to some degree including those older than four years. For example, if the price of young cars (newer than four years) decreases, some buyers of cars that are only slightly older than four years can afford young cars for the same price. Hence, the demand and prices for cars slightly older than four years could decrease as well. Similarly, for cars that are only slightly newer than a clunker and therefore not suitable for scrapping, prices could slightly increase because these cars are potential substitutes for old clunkers. To sum up, the reference group may be influenced by groups of cars that are positively and negatively affected by the scrappage premium due to spillover effects. However, it is expected that these price effects are rather small and can possibly offset each other. Nonetheless, the previous regression analyses of Section 5.6.1 will be repeated defining large cars older than four years and newer than 6.9 years as the new reference group.[133] By doing so, the reference group is not affected by positive price effects by the substitutes of clunkers. As the possibility that the prices of the substitutes of young cars do not decrease cannot be certainly excluded, at least the additional price effect for young cars can be measured. Thus, the following results measure rather the lower bound of the true effect whereas the obtained results from Section 5.6 are the best estimates. Table 5.13 shows the results of the regression analyses.

Table 5.14 shows the resulting difference-in-differences estimators of each regression. The same design as in Table 5.7 is used. The significance levels are determined using the Wald test.

The difference-in-difference estimators do not differ much from the estimators in Table 5.8. As expected, they are slightly greater in the short-run, but this effect is very small (only 0.1-0.2 percentage points). Surprisingly, the difference-in-differences estimators are slightly lower in the medium-run, but except of prices of households' car advertisements this effect is relatively small (0.4 percentage points). Hence, these results support the robustness of the obtained findings regarding hypotheses H1a and H1b.

---

[133] The value 6.9 is chosen because it is the median of the age of the old reference group.

Table 5.13: **Robustness Checks: Effect of Scrappage for Small Young Cars**
This table lists the results of OLS regressions with robust standard errors for the data set of the Internet platform of used cars. Small young cars are employed as the treatment group and large cars that are only slightly older as the reference group. Regressions (E.1) and (E.2) show the results for the differences between the period of the subsidy prior to the increase in the budget (Q1/2009) and the period after the increase (scrappage2) for the complete sample, regressions (E.3) and (E.4) show the results only for the dealers' sales offerings and (E.5) and (E.6) only show the results for private advertisements. The regressions are divided into a short-run effect (scrappage2=1 if the sales date fell in Q2 or Q3/2009) and a medium-run effect (scrappage2=1 if the sales date fell between Q2/2009 and Q4/2010). The robust standard errors are reported in parentheses. The symbols †,*,** and ***, indicate statistical significance at the 10% level, 5% level, 1% level and 0.1% level, respectively.

	(E.1)	(E.2)	(E.3)	(E.4)	(E.5)	(E.6)
	Full sample		Dealer		Private	
	Short-run	Medium-run	Short-run	Medium-run	Short-run	Medium-run
Scrappage2	-0.013***	-0.008***	-0.014***	-0.010***	-0.004	-0.009***
	(0.000)	(0.000)	(0.000)	(0.000)	(0.137)	(0.000)
Scrappage2 × Small	0.008***	-0.008***	0.009***	-0.005**	-0.004	-0.025***
	(0.000)	(0.000)	(0.000)	(0.009)	(0.473)	(0.000)
Scrappage2 × Young	-0.003**	0.001	-0.001	0.003***	-0.012**	-0.008*
	(0.004)	(0.133)	(0.146)	(0.000)	(0.002)	(0.013)
Scrappage2 × Small × Young	-0.011***	-0.005*	-0.012***	-0.008**	-0.003	-0.015*
	(0.000)	(0.021)	(0.000)	(0.002)	(0.713)	(0.043)
Small	-0.108***	-0.098***	-0.105***	-0.095***	-0.118***	-0.103***
	(0.000)	(0.000)	(0.000)	(0.000)	(0.000)	(0.000)
Young	0.001	-0.007***	0.002†	-0.008***	0.006	0.005
	(0.272)	(0.000)	(0.099)	(0.000)	(0.118)	(0.157)
Small × Young	-0.027***	-0.026***	-0.030**	-0.029***	-0.027**	-0.028**
	(0.000)	(0.000)	(0.000)	(0.000)	(0.006)	(0.002)
Private_Sale	-0.061***	-0.054***				
	(0.000)	(0.000)				
Constant	9.008***	9.018***	8.946***	8.965***	8.931***	8.930***
	(0.000)	(0.000)	(0.000)	(0.000)	(0.000)	(0.000)
Car-specific controls	Yes	Yes	Yes	Yes	Yes	Yes
Observations	1,141,240	2,533,962	1,061,592	2,332,803	79,648	201,159
R^2	0.852	0.862	0.852	0.863	0.834	0.840
Adjusted R^2	0.852	0.862	0.852	0.863	0.834	0.840

Table 5.14: **Robustness Checks: Effect of Scrappage for Small Young Cars (DiD)**
This table lists the difference-in-differences estimators using small young cars as the treatment and large cars that are only slightly older as the reference group. Using the Wald test, the symbols *,** and ***, indicate statistical significance at the 5% level, 1% level and 0.1% level, respectively.

	(E.1)	(E.2)	(E.3)	(E.4)	(E.5)	(E.6)
	Full sample		Dealer		Private	
	Short-run	Medium-run	Short-run	Medium-run	Short-run	Medium-run
Diff-in-diff estimator	-0.56%***	-1.16%***	-0.44%**	-1.00%***	-1.26%*	-1.79%***

5.7.2 Alternative Reference Group - Shortage of Old Clunkers

Again, the reference group is changed to control for possibly negatively affected prices of substitutes of young cars. The new reference group used for this robustness check only consists of cars that are not clunkers and older than the median of the age of the old reference group.[134] The regression results are listed in Table 5.15.

Table 5.15: **Robustness Checks: Effect of Scrappage for Clunkers**
This table lists the results of OLS regressions with robust standard errors for the data set of the Internet platform of used cars. Clunkers as defined in Table 5.4 are used as the treatment group and slightly young cars as the reference group. Regressions (F.1) and (F.2) show the results for the differences between the period of the subsidy prior to the increase in the budget (Q1/2009) and the period after the increase (scrappage2) for the complete sample, regressions (F.3) and (F.4) show the results for dealers' sales offerings and (F.5) and (F.6) show the results for private advertisements. The regressions are divided into a short-run effect (scrappage2=1 if the sales date fell in Q2 or Q3/2009) and a medium-run effect (scrappage2=1 if the sales date fell between Q2/2009 and Q4/2010). The robust standard errors are reported in parentheses. The symbols †,*,** and ***, indicate statistical significance at the 10% level, 5% level, 1% level and 0.1% level, respectively.

	(F.1)	(F.2)	(F.3)	(F.4)	(F.5)	(F.6)
	Full sample		Dealer		Private	
	Short-run	Medium-run	Short-run	Medium-run	Short-run	Medium-run
Scrappage2	-0.004***	-0.007***	-0.005***	-0.008***	-0.004	-0.009***
	(0.001)	(0.000)	(0.000)	(0.000)	(0.103)	(0.000)
Clunker	-0.299***	-0.287***	-0.324***	-0.323***	-0.243***	-0.224***
	(0.000)	(0.000)	(0.000)	(0.000)	(0.000)	(0.000)
Scrappage2 × Clunker	0.029***	0.039***	0.025***	0.054***	0.031***	0.022***
	(0.000)	(0.000)	(0.000)	(0.000)	(0.000)	(0.000)
Private_Sale	-0.068***	-0.076***				
	(0.000)	(0.000)				
Constant	9.548***	9.534***	9.433***	9.427***	9.438***	9.423***
	(0.000)	(0.000)	(0.000)	(0.000)	(0.000)	(0.000)
Car-specific controls	Yes	Yes	Yes	Yes	Yes	Yes
Observations	450,420	1,105,792	316,777	752,876	133,643	352,916
R^2	0.776	0.782	0.776	0.781	0.765	0.774
Adjusted R^2	0.776	0.782	0.776	0.781	0.765	0.774

Table 5.16 shows the resulting difference-in-differences estimators. The significance levels are determined using the Wald test.

The results confirm the hypotheses H2a and H2b. Highly significant positive estimators are observed, which are only slightly smaller than the estimators in Table 5.10 (0.3-

---

[134]The median of the age of all cars of the old reference group is 6.9.

Table 5.16: **Robustness Checks: Effect of Scrappage for Clunkers (DiD)**
This table lists the difference-in-differences estimators using clunkers as defined in Table 5.4 as the treatment and slightly newer cars as the reference group. The symbols *,** and ***, indicate statistical significance at the 5% level, 1% level and 0.1% level, respectively.

	(F.1)	(F.2)	(F.3)	(F.4)	(F.5)	(F.6)
	Full sample		Dealer		Private	
	Short-run	Medium-run	Short-run	Medium-run	Short-run	Medium-run
Diff-in-diff estimator	2.92%***	3.89%***	2.51%***	5.42%***	3.13%***	2.24%***

0.5 percentage points). Because some cars of the reference group may be substitutes of clunkers, their prices may be affected by the scrappage scheme. Hence, it can be concluded that the observed price effect in Table 5.16 is likely to be even greater.

5.8 Interim Results

Governments can influence market activity by supporting particular industries or promoting specific market behaviors. Typical examples are the financial support of forward-looking technologies and renewable energies. Generally, these interventions are aimed at promoting economic and social policy. For example, government subsidies such as accelerated vehicle retirement programs are frequently employed as political instruments to stabilize or stimulate the economy because the automotive sector is very important in many developed countries. Its large share of the respective gross domestic product (GDP) and spillover effects and linkages to other branches emphasize the relevance of this industry. Former studies focused on the effect of subsidies on the primary market or subsidized companies. Few studies have addressed the effects of these political interventions on the secondary markets and whether subsidies affect the prices of used durable goods. In addition, these studies do not distinguish between different car segments. Using the example of the German accelerated vehicle retirement program in 2009, this study fills this gap in the literature by analyzing the price effect of supply and demand shocks caused by government subsidies and scrappage programs on secondary markets taking different car segments into account. A data set of more than 16,000 sales results of used cars, which were provided by a large German leasing company, and a second data set of over 3.6 million sales advertisements from AutoScout24, which is one of the largest German Internet platforms of used cars, are employed to perform regression analyses using difference-in-differences estimation techniques.

It can be determined that the effects of the scrappage premium strongly depend on the car segment. The used-car prices of young vehicles of small car segments substantially depreciate compared with other segments that were not or only slightly affected by the scrappage scheme. A maximum price decline of five percentage points can be measured in the short-run and a maximum price decline of ten percentage points in the medium-run. After expiration of the program, the used-car prices of the small car segments were significantly less than the prices prior to the scrappage scheme and even significantly less than the prices during the subsidy. This shows that such programs affect the secondary market prices not only during the period of the accelerated vehicle retirement program but also for a longer time horizon.

Furthermore, it was analyzed whether the shortage of clunkers, which were scrapped and left the used-car market, affects used-car prices of old low-cost cars. The obtained findings confirm this assumption because increasing prices up to six percentage points could be found. This notion confirms that many low-income households even lose wealth due to the scrappage program.

It can be concluded that the secondary market is affected by welfare losses that are caused by a demand shock for small young cars and a low supply of old clunkers, which should be considered when analyzing the total welfare effect of scrappage schemes. This reveals an interesting issue for future research.

Additionally, it was found evidence that private car holders of old clunkers rationally offered their cars at higher prices to compensate for losing the option of scrapping their old cars and receiving a premium.

Finally, it was obtained evidence of information asymmetries in the secondary market and it can be inferred that car dealers have superior abilities to assess prices according to the developments of the market, but this effect is mainly relevant for the segment of old clunkers because this market is substantially smaller and less transparent.

5.9 Appendix

5.9.1 Difference-in-Differences Estimator

The difference-in-differences estimation technique is a useful method to evaluate the effect of a policy or another certain event for pooled cross-sectional data. Two pooled cross-sectional data sets, which cover the period before and after the occurrence of the policy, are needed to determine the effect of the event. The data sets of both periods have to contain information about a treatment group, which is assumed to be affected by the policy, and a control group that is not affected by the event. Then, the effect of the event can be determined by the different reaction of the treatment group and the control group. This method allows to control for other effects such as the economic development, which have the same impact on both groups.

More formally, consider the following regression model, where C is defined as the control group and T as the treatment group. The dummy variable dT equals one if the observation belongs to T, and zero otherwise. The post-policy period is indicated by d2. The variable of interest can be modeled by

$$y = \beta_0 + \delta_0 d2 + \beta_1 dT + \delta_1 d2 \cdot dT + \gamma' X + u, \tag{5.11}$$

where the vector X contains all control variables and u is the error term.[135] The effect of the policy is measured by the coefficient δ_1, which is the difference-in-differences estima-

---

[135] See Wooldridge (2016, p. 407 ff.).

tor. Without considering other factors such as the control variables X, the difference-in-differences estimator $\hat{\delta}_1$ can be obtained by

$$\hat{\delta}_1 = (\bar{y}_{2,T} - \bar{y}_{2,C}) - (\bar{y}_{1,T} - \bar{y}_{1,C}). \tag{5.12}$$

The first subscript indicates if the period is before (index equals 1) or after (index equals 2) the occurrence of the event and the second subscript denotes the group. The following table gives an overview about the general difference-in-differences setup:[136]

Table 5.17: **Policy Effect for the Treatment Group and Control Group**

	Before	**After**	**After-Before**
Control	β_0	$\beta_0 + \delta_0$	δ_0
Treatment	$\beta_0 + \beta_1$	$\beta_0 + \delta_0 + \beta_1 + \delta_1$	$\delta_0 + \delta_1$
Treatment – Control	β_1	$\beta_1 + \delta_1$	δ_1

5.9.2 Wald-Test

An established method for hypothesis testing is the Wald test. Due to the derived hypotheses of this chapter, it is focused on linear hypothesis testing, which means that hypotheses can be expressed by a linear combination of parameters, for example $H_0 : \beta_2 = 0$ and $H_0 : \beta_2 - \beta_3 - 5 = 0$. Joint hypotheses testing considers both hypotheses simultaneously.[137]

Generally, this can be expressed by the following linear combination:

$$H_0 : \mathbf{R}\beta - \mathbf{r} = 0$$
$$H_1 : \mathbf{R}\beta - \mathbf{r} \neq 0 \tag{5.13}$$

where $\mathbf{R}$ is an $h \times k$ matrix, $\mathbf{r}$ is an $h \times 1$ vector, $h \leq k$, h is the number of hypotheses and k is the number of parameters. Then, the Wald test tests if the expression $\mathbf{R}\hat{\beta} - \mathbf{r}$ is

---

[136]Following Wooldridge (2016, p. 410 f.).
[137]See Cameron and Trivedi (2010, p. 403 ff.).

significantly different from zero. As the distribution of $\hat{\beta}_i$ is normal, a linear combination of normal distributed variables is normal. It can therefore be concluded that under H_0

$$\mathbf{R}\hat{\beta} - \mathbf{r} \overset{a}{\sim} \mathcal{N}(0, \mathbf{R}Var(\hat{\beta})\mathbf{R}'). \tag{5.14}$$

As only single hypothesis is tested in these analyses, $\mathbf{R}\hat{\beta} - \mathbf{r}$ simplifies into a scalar that is univariate normally distributed. Hence, the Z-test can be applied. For multiple hypotheses, under H_0, the Wald statistic W for the test of $H_0 : \mathbf{R}\hat{\beta} - \mathbf{r}$ is:

$$W = (\mathbf{R}\hat{\beta} - \mathbf{r})' \left\{ \mathbf{R}\hat{V}(\hat{\beta})\mathbf{R}' \right\}^{-1} (\mathbf{R}\hat{\beta} - \mathbf{r}) \overset{a}{\sim} \chi^2(h), \tag{5.15}$$

where $\hat{V}(\hat{\beta})$ is a consistent estimate for $Var(\hat{\beta})$. Choosing a significance level α, H_0 will be rejected if the p-value

$$p = P(\chi^2(h) > W) < \alpha \tag{5.16}$$

or if W is greater than the critical value $c = \chi^2_\alpha(h)$.

6 Conclusion

At the beginning of this thesis, an overview about the German automobile and leasing market was given. Special attention has been drawn on vehicle leasing and the used-car market because of their substantial and increasing market share in recent years. This development and the intensified regulatory requirements following the financial crisis in 2007-2008 increased the importance of an adequate residual value risk management for financial institutions that are involved in the leasing business and vehicle financing. Hence, it is essential to identify all relevant factors that determine the prices of used vehicles to understand the price developments in the secondary car market.

Against this background, Chapter 3 presents an literature overview about determinants of residual values. The results of manifold studies show that there are many different factors that can affect the prices of used automobiles. All in all, vehicles decrease approximately by an exponential depreciation rate over life. The highest explanatory power was verifiable for physical attributes. Physical and car-specific characteristics have a significant impact on the used-car prices: on the one hand, the brand's reliability and supplementary equipment can increase the automobile's residual value. On the other hand, car age, mileage and the fuel consumption can be identified as value-reducing factors in particular. Additionally, the developments in the car markets are important to explain changes in the secondary market prices over time. Relevant factors are the introduction of new model lines and gasoline prices. Furthermore, there is a strong interaction between the primary and secondary market so that changes in the primary market such as the number of new registrations directly affect automobiles' residual values. Changes in the macro-economic environment except for changes in the fuel prices have minor impact on cars' prices. Only for the small car segments price effects are observable.

However, besides the wide range of the identified determinants of residual values from the literature, the market value of the leased vehicles at the end of the leased term can also be affected by other factors such as exogenous shocks resulting from a changed demand and supply behavior. Moreover, market participants' willingness to pay can differ from model-based expectations because individuals do not always behave rational and are less well informed about the developments in the used-car market and all relevant details that determine the price of the offered car. Two empirical research projects have addressed the price effect of these described influencing factors, which have rather been neglected in the literature, on the used-car's market value.

In Chapter 4, it was empirically shown that individuals' price assessment can substantially differ from rational model-based prices due to limited and heuristic information processing. For this reason, the market prices of lease returns may be greater or lower than their contractual residual values. Against this background, the effect of individuals' heuristic information processing on their car valuation was investigated. In the empirical analyses, a data set of approximately seven million used-car advertisements from AutoScout24 was used. Analyzing infra-annual price effects regarding the year of a car's initial registration, it was found that individuals tend to anchor on the average car value of similar cars of the same vintage. This results in higher prices of cars that were first-time registered early in a year than those of cars registered late in a year. Hence, the price difference of two similar cars that only differ in their month of the initial registration can be substantial. Furthermore, it was found that the size of the anchoring effect depends on seller's level of information and cognitive abilities. Well-informed market participants such as professional car dealers are aware of individuals' heuristic information processing and deliberately exploit anchoring for their own profit. Compared to car advertisements of private sellers, it was shown that the size of the anchoring effect of professional sellers is greater if the car was initially registered in the first half of a year and lower if the car was initially registered in the second half of a year. The size of the anchoring effect decreases with increasing cognitive abilities. For car advertisements of low-income and poorly-educated households this effect is more pronounced.

Financial institutions that are involved in the leasing business or vehicle financing can benefit from these results. On the one hand, the residual value risk increases if there exists a concentration of leased vehicles that were first-time registered in the second half of a year. This is often the case for fleet leasing. On the other hand, the risk and the required capital decreases if the leased vehicles were mostly first-time registered in the first half of a year. Moreover, the obtained results are also relevant for buyers and sellers of both new and used cars. For example, buyers of new cars should register their car in the first half of year if they want to resale the car at a later point in time. Buyers of used-cars should decide for a car initially registered in the second half of a year. In addition, these findings should also be used for price negotiations and the valuation of used cars.

In Chapter 5, the price effects of supply and demand shocks in the used-car market were empirically analyzed. For this purpose, a data set of more than 16,000 lease returns was employed, which were provided by a large German leasing company, and a second data set of approximately 3.6 million sales advertisement from AutoScout24, Europe's largest Internet platform of used cars. These data sets cover the time period from October 2008 to December 2010. In the focus of the investigation was the German scrappage scheme, which was implemented in 2009. This governmental intervention subsidized consumers for purchasing a new car and scrapping an old fuel-inefficient clunker. As a result, the scrappage scheme caused a change in the demand and supply in the used-car market. It was found that the effects strongly depend on the car segment. Using difference-in-differences methods, it was shown that the prices of low-priced young used cars decline due to a decreasing demand and the prices of low-priced old cars increased due to a decreasing supply. Even after the expiration of the scrappage program, the used-car prices of the affected car segments were significantly lower than during the subsidy. It can therefore be concluded that supply and demand shocks do not only exhibit a short-term price effect but rather persist for a longer time horizon.

These results are beneficial for several market participants. It is essential for financial institutions, which are exposed to the residual value risk, to adjust their risk assessment and forecasts about the future residual values of their leased vehicles. Otherwise, their residual value forecasts are biased and the risk could be underestimated. Governments can also benefit from the obtained results. Accelerated vehicle retirement programs are frequently employed as political instruments to stimulate the economy. Current issues, such as air pollution and the sales of electric vehicles illustrate the relevance of these analyses. The obtained results help to evaluate the total welfare effects of scrappage schemes because it can be concluded that the welfare losses in the secondary market can be substantial for some market participants.

Furthermore, the empirical study has provided insights into the functioning and price-formation process on secondary markets with heterogeneous sellers. First, private car holders of old clunkers offered their cars at higher prices because they want to be compensated for loosing their option of scrapping their old cars and receiving a premium. Second, professional car dealers have superior abilities to assess prices according to the development of the market because they are better informed than private sellers and can benefit from their experience. This gives evidence for information asymmetries in the used-car market.

In this thesis, several aspects in the context of residual value determinants have been highlighted and analyzed. However, there is still room for further analyses. An extension of the detailed data set from AutoScout24 that also covers the time period before the announcement of the German scrappage scheme may be useful to verify these results. This would provide a clear distinction of the time prior to the introduction of the subsidy and the scrappage scheme. Moreover, increasing number of observations prior to the year 2009 would improve the quality and provide informative results about the magnitude of the estimated price effect. In this context, another aspect is the question whether the used control group for the baseline scenario is a good choice in the difference-in-difference approach. As explained in Chapter 5, the control group may be slightly affected by the scrappage premium. Another approach to measure the effect of the scrappage scheme, could employ a panel data set of used-car prices on a country and segment level. Then, e.g., synthetic control methods can be applied to obtain an appropriate control group. However, the problem is to find adequate time series about car prices that also take into account the same car classification. These can vary significantly between countries. Finally, the obtained results may also suffer from unobserved variables. Thus, the implementation of other car-specific variables like the color or the equipment should be useful to strengthen the results.

Bibliography

Ackerman, S. R. (1973). Used cars as a depreciating asset. *Economic Inquiry*, 11(4):463–474.

Adda, J. and Cooper, R. (2000). Balladurette and Juppette: A Discrete Analysis of Scrapping Subsidies. *Journal of Political Economy*, 108(4):778–806.

Akaike, H. (1974). A New Look at the Statistical Model Identification. *IEEE Transactions on Automatic Control*, 19(6):716–723.

Akerlof, G. (1976). The Economics of Caste and of the Rat Race and other Woeful Tales. *Quarterly Journal of Economics*, 90(4):599–617.

Akerlof, G. A. (1970). The Market for "Lemons": Quality Uncertainty and the Market Mechanism. *Quarterly Journal of Economics*, 84(3):488–500.

Alberini, A., Harrington, W., and McConnell, V. (1995). Determinants of participation in accelerated vehicle-retirement programs. *RAND Journal of Economics*, 26(1):93–112.

Alberini, A., Harrington, W., and McConnell, V. (1996). Estimating an Emissions Supply Function from Accelerated Vehicle Retirement Programs. *Review of Economics and Statistics*, 78(2):251–265.

Andreoni, J. and Bergstrom, T. (1996). Do government subsidies increase the private supply of public goods? *Public Choice*, 88(3-4):295–308.

Andrews, T. and Benzing, C. (2007). The determinants of price in internet auctions of used cars. *Atlantic Economic Journal*, 35(1):43–57.

Angrist, J. and Pischke, J.-S. (2009). *Mostly Harmless Econometrics*. Princeton.

Basu, K. (1997). Why are so many goods priced to end in nine? And why this practice hurts the producers. *Economics Letters*, 54(1):41–44.

Basu, K. (2006). Consumer Cognition and Pricing in the Nines in Oligopolistic Markets. *Journal of Economics & Management Strategy*, 15(1):125–141.

Bennett, W. B. (1967). Cross-section Studies of the Consumption of Automobiles in the United States. *The American Economic Review*, 57(4):841–850.

Bergman, O., Ellingsen, T., Johannesson, M., and Svensson, C. (2010). Anchoring and cognitive ability. *Economics Letters*, 107(1):66–68.

Bergström, F. (2000). Capital Subsidies and the Performance of Firms. *Small Business Economics*, 14(3):183–193.

Berry, S., Levinsohn, J., and Pakes, A. (1995). Automobile Prices in Market Equilibrium. *Econometrica*, 63(4):841–890.

Betts, S. C. and Taran, Z. (2004). The'brand halo'effect on durable goods prices: Brand reliability and the used car market. *Academy of Marketing Studies Journal*, 8(1):7.

Böckers, V., Heimeshoff, U., and Müller, A. (2012). Pull-forward effects in the German car scrappage scheme: A time series approach. *DICE Discussion Paper 56*.

Bond, E. W. (1982). A Direct Test of the "Lemons" Model: The Market for Used Pickup Trucks. *American Economic Review*, 72(4):836–840.

Brown, J., Hossain, T., and Morgan, J. (2010). Shrouded Attributes and Information Suppression: Evidence from the Field. *Quarterly Journal of Economics*, 125(2):859–876.

Busse, M. R., Knittel, C. R., Silva-Risso, J., and Zettelmeyer, F. (2012). Did "Cash for Clunkers" Deliver? The Consumer Effects of the Car Allowance Rebate System. *Working Paper*.

Busse, M. R., Knittel, C. R., and Zettelmeyer, F. (2009). Pain at the pump: how gasoline prices affect automobile purchasing in new and used markets. *NBER working paper*, 15590.

Busse, M. R., Knittel, C. R., and Zettelmeyer, F. (2013a). Are consumers myopic? Evidence from new and used car purchases. *American Economic Review*, 103(1):220–56.

Busse, M. R., Lacetera, N., Pope, D. G., Silva-Risso, J., and Sydnor, J. R. (2013b). Estimating the Effect of Salience in Wholesale and Retail Car Markets. *American Economic Review*, 103(3):575–579.

Cameron, A. and Trivedi, P. (2010). *Microeconometrics Using Stata*. Stata Press. Revised Edition.

Cantos-Sánchez, P., Gutiérrez-i Puigarnau, E., and Mulalic, I. (2018). The impact of scrappage programmes on the demand for new vehicles: Evidence from spain. *Research in Transportation Economics*, 70:83–96.

Chen, J., Esteban, S., and Shum, M. (2010). Do sales tax credits stimulate the automobile market? *International Journal of Industrial Organization*, 28(4):397–402.

Chen, J., Esteban, S., and Shum, M. (2013). When Do Secondary Markets Harm Firms? *American Economic Review*, 103(7):2911–2934.

Cheng, B. and Wu, X. (2006). A modified PLSR method in prediction. *J. Data Science*, 4:257–274.

Chetty, R., Looney, A., and Kroft, K. (2009). Salience and Taxation: Theory and Evidence. *American Economic Review*, 99(4):1145–1177.

Das, S. (2009). *Perspectives on financial services*. Allied Publishers Pvt. Ltd.

De Long, J. B. and Summers, L. H. (1991). Equipment Investment and Economic Growth. *Quarterly Journal of Economics*, 106(2):445–502.

DellaVigna, S. and Pollet, J. M. (2009). Investor Inattention and Friday Earnings Announcements. *Journal of Finance*, 64(2):709–749.

Deng, H. and Ma, A. C. (2010). Market Structure and Pricing Strategy of China's Automobile Industry. *The Journal of Industrial Economics*, 58(4):818–845.

Deutsche Automobil Treuhand (2016). DAT-Report 2016. `https://www.dat.de/fileadmin/user_upload/DAT-Report_2016.pdf`. Accessed March 25, 2018.

Dexheimer, V. (2003). Hedonic methods of price measurement for used cars. *Technical Report, German Federal Statistical Office*.

Dill, J. (2004). Estimating emissions reductions from accelerated vehicle retirement programs. *Transportation Research Part D: Transport and Environment*, 9(2):87–106.

Dunham, W. R. (1997). Are automobile safety regulations worth the price: Evidence from used car markets. *Economic inquiry*, 35(3):579–589.

Engers, M., Hartmann, M., and Stern, S. (2009). Annual miles drive used car prices. *Journal of Applied Econometrics*, 24(1):1–33.

Englmaier, F. and Schmöller, A. (2010). Determinants and Effects of Reserve Prices in Hattrick Auctions. *Discussion Paper No. 326*.

Englmaier, F., Schmöller, A., and Stowasser, T. (2017). Price discontinuities in an online market for used cars. *Management Science*, 64(6):2754–2766.

Esteban, S. (2007). Effective Scrappage Subsidies. *BE Journal of Theoretical Economics*, 7(1):1–32.

Esteban, S. and Shum, M. (2007). Durable-goods oligopoly with secondary markets: the case of automobiles. *RAND Journal of Economics*, 38(2):332–354.

European Commission (2002). *Distribution and Serving of Motor Vehicles in the European Union - Explanatory Brochure*. European Commission Regulation No. 1400/2002, Brüssel.

Federal Motor Transport Authority (2012). Monatliche Neuzulassungen. https://www.kba.de/DE/Statistik/Fahrzeuge/Neuzulassungen/MonatlicheNeuzulassungen/2008_2013/2008_2013_node.html. Accessed March 01, 2018.

Federal Motor Transport Authority (2016). Personenkraftwagen am 1. Januar 2016 nach ausgewählten Merkmalen. https://www.kba.de/DE/Statistik/Fahrzeuge/Bestand/Ueberblick/2016/2016_b_barometer.html?nn=1592204. Accessed March 25, 2018.

Federal Motor Transport Authority (2017a). Besitzumschreibungen. https://www.kba.de/DE/Statistik/Fahrzeuge/Besitzumschreibungen/besitzumschreibungen_node.html. Accessed March 25, 2018.

Federal Motor Transport Authority (2017b). Neuzulassungen. https://www.kba.de/DE/Statistik/Fahrzeuge/Neuzulassungen/neuzulassungen_node.html. Accessed March 25, 2018.

Federal Motor Transport Authority (2017c). Neuzulassungen von Personenkraftwagen im Dezember 2016 nach Segmenten und Modellreihen. https://www.kba.de/SharedDocs/Publikationen/DE/Statistik/Fahrzeuge/FZ/2016_monatlich/FZ11/fz11_2016_12_pdf.pdf?__blob=publicationFile&v=2. Accessed March 25, 2018.

Federal Office of Economics and Export Control (2009). Richtlinie zur Förderung des Absatzes von Personenkraftwagen. http://www.alfersgmbh.de/DOWNLOADS/RS%2023%2003%202009%20Anlage.pdf. Accessed March 30, 2017.

Federal Office of Economics and Export Control (2010). Abschlussbericht - Umweltprämie. https://www.yumpu.com/de/document/view/7498784/abschlussbericht-umweltpramie-bafa. Accessed March 30, 2017.

Federation of German Leasing Companies (2016). Leasing 2016. https://bdl.leasingverband.de/internet/downloads/Berichte/Jahresberichte/bdl-jahresbericht-2016.pdf. Accessed March 15, 2017.

Federation of German Leasing Companies (2017). Jahres- und Strukturdaten. https://bdl.leasingverband.de/zahlen-fakten/leasing-in-deutschland/jahres-und-strukturdaten/. Accessed February 4, 2017.

Finkelstein, A. (2009). E-ztax: Tax Salience and Tax Rates. *Quarterly Journal of Economics*, 124(3):969–1010.

Gavazza, A., Lizzeri, A., and Roketskiy, N. (2014). A Quantitative Analysis of the Used-Car Market. *American Economic Review*, 104(11):3668–3700.

Gilbert, T., Kogan, S., Lochstoer, L., and Ozyildirim, A. (2012). Investor Inattention and the Market Impact of Summary Statistics. *Management Science*, 58(2):336–350.

Gilmore, E. A. and Lave, L. B. (2013). Comparing resale prices and total cost of ownership for gasoline, hybrid and diesel passenger cars and trucks. *Transport Policy*, 27:200–208.

Gilovich, T., Griffin, D., and Kahneman, D. (2002). *Heuristics and Biases: The Psychology of Intuitive Judgment*. Cambridge University Press.

Goodman, A. C. (1983). Willingness to pay for car efficiency: A hedonic price approach. *Journal of Transport Economics and Policy*, 17:247–266.

Gordon, R. J. (1990). *The Measurement of Durable Goods Prices*. University of Chicago Press.

Grigolon, L., Leheyda, N., and Verboven, F. (2016). Scrapping Subsidies During the Financial Crisis – Evidence from Europe. *International Journal of Industrial Organization*, 44:41–59.

Grossman, S. J. and Stiglitz, J. E. (1980). On the Impossibility of Informationally Efficient Markets. *American Economic Review*, 70(3):393–408.

Gürtler, M. and Gutknecht, S. (2016). Exploiting Anchoring: The Advantage of Being a Professional Seller. *Working Paper*.

Gürtler, M., Gutknecht, S., and Hibbeln, M. T. (2016). The Price Effect of Supply and Demand Shocks on Secondary Markets - Evidence from the 'Cash-for-Clunkers' Program in Germany. *Working Paper*.

Hahn, R. W. (1995). An Economic Analysis of Scrappage. *RAND Journal of Economics*, 26(2):222–242.

Hammond, R. G. (2013). Sudden unintended used-price deceleration? the 2009–2010 toyota recalls. *Journal of Economics & Management Strategy*, 22(1):78–100.

Hanemann, W. M. (1991). Willingness to Pay and Willingness to Accept: How Much Can They Differ? *American Economic Review*, 81(3):635–647.

Hartman, R. S. (1987). Product quality and market efficiency: The effect of product recalls on resale prices and firm valuation. *The Review of Economics and Statistics*, pages 367–372.

Haugh, D., Mourougane, A., and Chatal, O. (2010). The Automobile Industry in and Beyond the Crisis. *Working Paper*.

Heyd, R. (2008). Leasing im Bilanz und Steuerrecht. In von Westphalen, F. and Hansen, S. P., editors, *Der Leasingvertrag*. Köln.

Hirshleifer, D., Lim, S. S., and Teoh, S. H. (2009). Driven to Distraction: Extraneous Events and Underreaction to Earnings News. *Journal of Finance*, 64(5):2289–2325.

Hoekstra, M., Puller, S. L., and West, J. (2017). Cash for corollas: When stimulus reduces spending. *American Economic Journal: Applied Economics*, 9(3):1–35.

International Organization of Motor Vehicle Manufacturers (2017). PC world vehicles in use. http://www.oica.net/wp-content/uploads//PC_Vehicles-in-use.pdf. Accessed March 25, 2018.

Jacobsen, M. R. and Van Benthem, A. A. (2015). Vehicle scrappage and gasoline policy. *American Economic Review*, 105(3):1312–38.

Kagel, J. H. and Levin, D. (1986). The Winner's Curse and Public Information in Common Value Auctions. *American Economic Review*, 76(5):894–920.

Kahn, J. A. (1986). Gasoline prices and the used automobile market: a rational expectations asset price approach. *The Quarterly Journal of Economics*, 101(2):323–339.

Kahneman, D., Knetsch, J. L., and Thaler, R. H. (1991). Anomalies: The Endowment Effect, Loss Aversion, and Status Quo Bias. *Journal of Economic Perspectives*, 5(1):193–206.

Kandel, S., Sarig, O., and Wohl, A. (2001). Do Investors Prefer Round Stock Prices? Evidence from Israeli IPO Auctions. *Journal of Banking & Finance*, 25(8):1543–1551.

Kaul, A., Pfeifer, G., and Witte, S. (2012). The Incidence of Cash for Clunkers: An Analysis of the 2009 Car Scrappage Scheme in Germany. *Working Paper*.

Kavalec, C. and Setiawan, W. (1997). An analysis of accelerated vehicle retirement programs using a discrete choice personal vehicle model. *Transport Policy*, 4(2):95–107.

Kihm, A. and Vance, C. (2016). The determinants of equity transmission between the new and used car markets: a hedonic analysis. *Journal of the Operational Research Society*, 67(10):1250–1258.

Knittel, C. R. (2009). The Implied Cost of Carbon Dioxide Under the Cash for Clunkers Program. *SSRN Working Paper*.

Konishi, S. and Kitagawa, G. (2008). *Information Criteria and Statistical Modeling*. New York.

Kooreman, P. and Haan, M. A. (2006). Price Anomalies in the Used Car Market. *De Economist*, 154(1):41–62.

Korvorst, M. and Damian, M. F. (2008). The differential influence of decades and units on multidigit number comparison. *Quarterly Journal of Experimental Psychology*, 61(8):1250–1264.

Kraemer-Eis, H. and Lang, F. (2012). The importance of leasing for SME finance. Technical report, EIF Working Paper.

Kraftfahrt-Bundesamt (2016). Fahrzeugzulassungen (FZ). `https://www.kba.de/ SharedDocs/Publikationen/DE/Statistik/Fahrzeuge/FZ/2016/fz4_2016_pdf. pdf?__blob=publicationFile&v=2`. Accessed March 01, 2018.

Kratzer, J. and Kreuzmair, B. (2002). *Leasing in Theorie und Praxis*. Wiesbaden. 2nd edition.

Kwon, O., Dukes, A. J., Siddarth, S., and Silva-Risso, J. M. (2015). The Informational Role of Product Trade-Ins for Pricing Durable Goods. *The Journal of Industrial Economics*, 63(4):736–762.

Lacetera, N., Pope, D. G., and Sydnor, J. R. (2012). Heuristic Thinking and Limited Attention in the Car Market. *American Economic Review*, 102(5):2206–2236.

Leaseeurope (2015). Key Facts and Figures. `http://www.leaseurope.org/index.php? page=key-facts-figures`. Accessed March 15, 2017.

Lee, D. S. and Lemieux, T. (2010). Regression Discontinuity Designs in Economics. *Journal of Economic Literature*, 48(2):281–355.

Lenski, S. M., Keoleian, G. A., and Bolon, K. M. (2010). The impact of 'Cash for Clunkers' on greenhouse gas emissions: a life cycle perspective. *Environmental Research Letters*, 5(4):1–8.

Levin, D., Kagel, J. H., and Richard, J.-F. (1996). Revenue Effects and Information Processing in English Common Value Auctions. *American Economic Review*, 86(3):442–460.

Lewis, G. (2011). Asymmetric Information, Adverse Selection and Online Disclosure: The Case of eBay Motors. *American Economic Review*, 101(4):1535–1546.

Li, S., Linn, J., and Spiller, E. (2013). Evaluating "Cash-for-Clunkers": Program effect on auto sales and the environment. *Journal of Environmental Economics and Management*, 65(2):175–193.

List, J. A. (2003). Does Market Experience Eliminate Market Anomalies? *Quarterly Journal of Economics*, 118(1):41–72.

List, J. A. (2004). Neoclassical Theory Versus Prospect Theory: Evidence from the Marketplace. *Econometrica*, 72(2):615–625.

Lock, V. (2003). Review of the leasing and asset-finance industry. In Boobyer, C. L., editor, *Leasing and Asset Finance: The Comprehensive Guide for Practitioners*. London. 4th edition.

Majid, K. A. and Russell, C. A. (2015). Giving green a second thought: Modeling the value retention of green products in the secondary market. *Journal of Business Research*, 68(5):994–1002.

Malkiel, B. G. and Fama, E. F. (1970). Efficient Capital Markets: A Review of Theory and Empirical Work. *Journal of Finance*, 25(2):383–417.

Malmendier, U. and Lee, Y. H. (2011). The bidder's curse. *American Economic Review*, 101(2):749–787.

Martinek, M., Stoffels, M., and Wimmer-Leonhardt, S. (2008). *Leasinghandbuch*. München. 2nd edition.

Mian, A. and Sufi, A. (2012). The Effects of Fiscal Stimulus: Evidence from the 2009 Cash for Clunkers Program. *Quarterly Journal of Economics*, 127(3):1107–1142.

Mitra, S. and Webster, S. (2008). Competition in remanufacturing and the effects of government subsidies. *International Journal of Production Economics*, 111(2):287–298.

Morton, F. S., Silva-Risso, J., and Zettelmeyer, F. (2011). What matters in a price negotiation: Evidence from the U.S. auto retailing industry. *Quantitative Marketing and Economics*, 9(4):365–402.

Morton, F. S., Zettelmeyer, F., and Silva-Risso, J. (2001). Internet car retailing. *The Journal of Industrial Economics*, 49(4):501–519.

Müller, A. and Heimeshoff, U. (2013). Evaluating the causal effects of cash-for-clunkers programs in selected countries: Success or failure? *Beiträge zur Jahrestagung des Vereins für Socialpolitik 2013: Wettbewerbspolitik und Regulierung in einer globalen Wirtschaftsordnung - Session: Empirics: Markets and Media, No. F13-V3*.

Nau, K. (2012). An empirical analysis of residual value risk in automotive lease contracts. University Hohenheim, stuttgart. `http://opus.uni-hohenheim.de/volltexte/2012/722/`. Accessed March 30, 2017.

Ohta, M. (1987). Gasoline cost and hedonic price indexes of us used cars for 1970–1983 a note. *Journal of Business & Economic Statistics*, 5(4):521–528.

Ohta, M. and Griliches, Z. (1976). Automobile prices revisited: Extensions of the hedonic hypothesis. In Terleckyj, N. E., editor, *Household Production and Consumption*. NBER.

Ohta, M. and Griliches, Z. (1986). Automobile prices and quality: Did the gasoline price increases change consumer tastes in the us? *Journal of Business & Economic Statistics*, 4(2):187–198.

Peles, Y. C. (1988). On the depreciation of automobiles. *International Journal of Transport Economics/Rivista internazionale di economia dei trasporti*, 15(1):43–54.

Pfeifer, G. (2013). *Consumption Effects of Scrapping Schemes: Worldwide Scrappage Schemes With a Special Focus on Consumption in Germany*. Shaker, Herzogenrath.

Poltrock, S. E. and Schwartz, D. R. (1984). Comparative Judgments of Multidigit Numbers. *Journal of Experimental Psychology: Learning, Memory, and Cognition*, 10(1):32–45.

Pope, D. G. (2009). Reacting to rankings: Evidence from "America's Best Hospitals". *Journal of Health Economics*, 28(6):1154–1165.

Prado, S. M. (2009). The european used-car market at a glance: Hedonic resale price valuation in automotive leasing industry. *Economics Bulletin*, 29(3):2086–2099.

Prieto, M., Caemmerer, B., and Baltas, G. (2015). Using a hedonic price model to test prospect theory assertions: The asymmetrical and nonlinear effect of reliability on used car prices. *Journal of Retailing and Consumer Services*, 22:206–212.

Purohit, D. (1992). Exploring the relationship between the markets for new and used durable goods: The case of automobiles. *Marketing Science*, 11(2):154–167.

Reinking, K. (2012). *AutoLeasing und AutoFinanzierung*. Köln. 5th edition.

Reinking, K. and Eggert, C. (2014). *Der Autokauf: Rechtsfragen bei Kauf neuer und gebrauchter Kraftfahrzeuge sowie beim Leasing*. Köln. 12th edition.

Rode, D. C., Fischbeck, P. S., and Dean, S. R. (2002). Residual risk and the valuation of leases under uncertainty and limited information. *Journal of Structured and Project Finance*, 7:37–49.

Santelmann, L.-H. and Mehrgott, M. (2012). Automobiles Leasing in Deutschland. In Fittler, M. and Mudersbach, M., editors, *Leasing-Handbuch für die betriebliche Praxis*. Frankfurt am Main. 8th edition.

Schiraldi, P. (2011). Automobile replacement: a dynamic structural approach. *RAND Journal of Economics*, 42(2):266–291.

Shogren, J. F., Shin, S. Y., Hayes, D. J., and Kliebenstein, J. B. (1994). Resolving Differences in Willingness to Pay and Willingness to Accept. *American Economic Review*, 84(1):255–270.

Simon, H. A. (1955). A Behavioral Model of Rational Choice. *Quarterly Journal of Economics*, 69(1):99–118.

Smith, L. D. and Jin, B. (2007). Modeling exposure to losses on automobile leases. *Review of Quantitative Finance and Accounting*, 29(3):241–266.

Städtler, A. (2014). Leasinggeschäft wächst 2014 deutlich schneller als die Anlageinvestitionen - moderater Optimismus für 2015. *Ifo Schnelldienst*, 67(23):53–63.

Storchmann, K. (2004). On the depreciation of automobiles: An international comparison. *Transportation*, 31(4):371–408.

Tacke, H. R. (1999). *Leasing*. Stuttgart. 3rd edition.

Tadelis, S. and Zettelmeyer, F. (2015). Information Disclosure as a Matching Mechanism: Theory and Evidence from a Field Experiment. *American Economic Review*, 105(2):886–905.

Tversky, A. and Kahneman, D. (1974). Judgment under Uncertainty: Heuristics and Biases. *Science*, 185(4157):1124–1131.

Van Wee, B., Moll, H. C., and Dirks, J. (2000). Environmental impact of scrapping old cars. *Transportation Research Part D: Transport and Environment*, 5(2):137–143.

White, E. (2016). Global leasing report. *White Clarke Group*.

Witte, S. (2013). *Economic Effects of Cash for Clunkers: Germany's Scrappage Scheme and Its Effects on the Market and Prices*. Wissenschaftlicher Verlag Berlin.

Wooldridge, J. M. (2016). *Introductory Econometrics: A Modern Approach*. Cengage Learning, South-Western. 6th edition.

Wu, J.-D., Hsu, C.-C., and Chen, H.-C. (2009). An expert system of price forecasting for used cars using adaptive neuro-fuzzy inference. *Expert Systems with Applications*, 36(4):7809–7817.

Wykoff, F. C. (1970). Capital Depreciation in the Postwar Period: Automobiles. *Review of Economics and Statistics*, 52(2):168–172.

Zettelmeyer, F., Morton, F. S., and Silva-Risso, J. (2006). How the internet lowers prices: Evidence from matched survey and automobile transaction data. *Journal of marketing research*, 43(2):168–181.